TWELVE GREAT
SPIRITUAL WRITERS

Liz Hoare

D1448533

First published in Great Britain in 2020

Society for Promoting Christian Knowledge
36 Causton Street
London SW1P 4ST
www.spck.org.uk

The author and publisher have made every effort to ensure that the external website
and email addresses included in this book are correct and up to date at the time of going
to press. The author and publisher are not responsible for the content,
quality or continuing accessibility of the sites.

British Library Cataloguing-in-Publication Data
A catalogue record for this book is available from the British Library

ISBN 978-0-281-07936-0
eBook ISBN 978-0-281-07937-7

Typeset by Nord Compo
First printed in Great Britain by Jellyfish Print Solutions
Subsequently digitally printed in Great Britain

eBook by Nord Compo

Produced on paper from sustainable forests

In memory of Ruth Etchells, spiritual guide and writer,
who was influential at the major turning points in my life

Contents

Introduction

A book, too, can be a star, 'explosive material, capable of stirring up fresh life endlessly', a living fire to lighten the darkness, leading out into the expanding universe.
(Madeleine L'Engle[1])

At the back of our brains is a blaze of astonishment at our own existence. The object of the artistic and spiritual life is to dig for this sunrise of wonder.
(G. K. Chesterton[2])

The objective of this book is to get you reading in order to draw inspiration and nourishment for your soul from a selection of women writers who are at work today. It has been written out of the conviction that reading can be a spiritual practice that helps us to grow more deeply into the fullness of life promised by God in generosity towards us.

Books nurture us, but they also stretch us by encouraging us to think differently as we enter into the minds of others. A favourite author becomes a friend, even though we may never meet him or her. The final writer featured in this book, Mary Oliver, began an essay entitled 'My Friend Walt Whitman' with the words, 'In Ohio in the 1950s I had a few friends who kept me sane, alert and loyal to my own best and wildest inclinations.'[3] We converse with such book friends in our minds and want to introduce them to others. Some of my favourite authors are represented here and I would like to help you to get to know them and to think about what motivated them to write. While this book is not intended as a work of scholarship,

1

I have tried to represent each writer in her context and with close reference to what she is saying through her words on the page.

Their common ground is spirituality, so the first task is to define this slippery word and set some boundary markers for the purpose of what follows.

What is spirituality?

'Spirituality' has become something of a catch-all word that can be stretched to mean whatever we would like it to mean. Our postmodern world loves to detach words and concepts from their moorings to reinvent them. Spirituality for many people denotes a pick-and-mix approach to the spiritual realm and may or may not include Christian aspects of faith and belief.

I tend to preface 'spirituality' with 'Christian' to anchor it firmly within the Christian faith. Spirituality has to do with the Spirit of God. The New Testament talks about living according to the Spirit (Romans 8) or by the Spirit (Galatians 5). Spirituality has a dynamic quality about it, as metaphors for the Spirit suggest: wind blowing where it wills, water springing up or a dove in flight. It touches on what we believe but it cannot remain in the head. It has to affect every part of human life: head and heart, faith and practice. Spirituality could therefore be described as the transforming work of the Spirit in every aspect of the life of the believer.

The twentieth-century writer Dallas Willard regarded spirituality as the way in which human beings are alive to God in the material world here and now.[4] My own simple working definition is, 'How I live out what I believe about God.'

I consider myself to be a Christian who writes, but here I am not writing to 'rate' the authors included as to their orthodoxy. Rather I am interested in the kinds of questions their writing raises for anyone who is interested in the life of the spirit and life in the Spirit. Marilynne Robinson remarked in her novel *Gilead* that 'nothing true can be said about God from a posture of defence'.[5] While some writers represented here are more sure-footed around doctrinal boundaries, all would acknowledge the place of mystery and the need to live with questions in order to grow. I hope there is something for explorers here, however tentative, as well as for confident fellow disciples.

The next section surveys some of the ingredients of orthodox Christian spirituality. I acknowledge at the outset that there are different emphases and approaches among Christians, and the lists of ingredients themselves might vary somewhat as well.

Ingredients of spirituality

For Christians, spirituality involves not only beliefs but also practices that form us. Prayer is perhaps the most obvious activity that Christians engage in to communicate with God and sustain the inner life of the soul. There is plenty of material about prayer from all the authors included in this book. Some of the authors focus specifically on prayer and offer their own experiences of it, and even suggest ways we might go about it ourselves. Margaret Guenther is an example of this in her writing on spiritual direction. In other writers it is more implicit, even taken for granted, forming the backdrop of the material in hand. Anne Lamott writes about talking to God in the struggles she has lived through and occasionally records what she has said to God on different occasions. Ann Lewin's prayer poems meanwhile offer examples of carefully crafted words that provide a way of praying that all can recognize and make their own.

Christian spirituality is built on a God who is made known to us in different ways, chiefly through the incarnation of the Lord Jesus Christ, the living Word. The record of the Bible is key to meditating and working out what this means for human beings in a given time and place. How does God call us to live in the light of the revelation of Jesus Christ? Detaching ourselves from this anchor point leads to a subjective spirituality lacking in content and direction.

Benedicta Ward shows us how people have done this in the past in circumstances very remote from our own context and yet speaks directly into the questions that continue to face us now. Alison Morgan, conversely, has a multiplicity of examples from around the world of people who have been transformed by turning to Christ and becoming his followers. Devotional reading of the Bible thus forms another essential aspect of Christian spiritual life. The authors here engage with the Scriptures in different ways, and novels such as those of Marilynne Robinson complement explanatory books such as Alison Morgan's.

The question of who Jesus is and what he was like in his earthly life is explored in the writing of Sister Margaret Magdalen, who combines her reflections with prayer and practical discipleship, thus drawing together the person of Jesus, the place of the Bible and the development of the spiritual life through prayer in imaginative and integrated ways.

There is no place in Christian spirituality for an individualistic and privatized approach. The Christian life is not a personal improvement plan. The Church as the body of Christ demands that we learn to live and relate with others, but it is not always an easy road. A number of writers here wrestle with the Church in different ways. Barbara Brown Taylor, for example, is a well-known preacher who led a thriving church in the USA but drew back from her role in order to refocus on what really matters. The way her role as leader played out was not conducive to a spiritual life of depth and meaning, and left her exhausted and her inner resources spent. By contrast, Kathleen Norris tracks her journey back to church having left it as a teenager, and while her doubts have remained and form the questioning approach of much of her writing, she has found a spirituality that is rooted in belonging.

Closely allied with Church is worship, which focuses our attention away from ourselves and on God. Worship is not just about singing hymns in church, however, and for many Christians the joyful acknowledgement of God and who God is often comes out of doors in walking and contemplating the world. Annie Dillard, Mary Oliver and Kathleen Norris are among those who are gifted with the ability to pay attention to creation and find there rich stores of food for the soul as well as the challenge to embrace the world yet sit lightly to it. Human beings in the context of creation is a theme that almost all the writers touch on: Benedicta Ward on the desert, Ann Lewin on watching birds and Kathleen Norris on the Great Plains of North and South Dakota remind us of the impact of nature on human existence and how God now whispers, now thunders to us there.

Prayer, Scripture, Church, worship, creation: what else provides the ingredients for Christian spirituality? Most would insist on solitude and silence, for at least some of the time, in order to hear and respond to God. Whether it is the poet wrestling with words or a desert dweller in his cell alone with the Almighty, both are here. Study also plays a part, and a number of writers have produced books about writing and what it entails. Sarah Clarkson has written about reading and its joys as well as the way books form us. She is a keen advocate of inhabiting the world of books, which is the principle behind this text.

There are other ingredients, of course: sacraments, for example, which do not sit centre stage here, though they form the background to the writings of women such as Barbara Brown Taylor and Margaret Guenther, both ordained priests.

Genres of writing

Prayers, poems, sermons, reflections, creative writing: they are all here. There are riches untold, waiting to be discovered, in books that explore spirituality.

We tend to stay within our own comfort zones in what we read and there is value in that – there is enough in each genre to last a lifetime – but there are other pastures to taste and see, beyond our horizons, where we may also find stimuli to growth. I have learned that there is much to be gained from reading authors we do not always agree with.

All the writers here offer material to help us orientate ourselves towards God so that life is informed, enriched and encouraged to grow. The authors selected cover many different aspects of the spiritual life. It is not an exhaustive list by any means, but alongside the usual components that most people consider essential for spirituality, there are writers included who help us to think more widely about living lives that are rooted and grounded in the Trinitarian God of the Christian faith.

Spiritual growth entails putting roots down deep as well as reaching up towards heaven. It is exciting to meet people who have come to faith recently, often with no Christian background. A new Christian has so much to discover, so much to reconsider, so much to recalibrate. It is my hope that this collection of writers will expand horizons rather than constrict or constrain. They do not set out to tell us how to live. Instead they offer invitations to see things with the eye of faith. They draw on the Christian tradition through writers who recorded their experiences of God in earlier times and places, but they express their thoughts in contemporary ways. Some of their sources became classics that are still read for their wisdom and insight. It may be a little early to say which of the writers represented here will become classics themselves, but who knows? Many of them deserve to be.

Choosing authors

Choosing who to include has not been easy. Some genres of writing could easily have filled the book. Women poets especially proved a difficult choice, not least because the one selected, Mary Oliver, died during the writing of the book. I decided to keep her because of her impact on modern poetry and her thoughts on the role of poetry in human life and experience.

Having been forced to omit many brilliant writers owing to lack of space, I hope that the discovery of a new author will encourage readers to explore further. One thing leads to another in reading. It might, for example, lead to the thought that if, say, poetry can help me pray, then art might do the same. Some genres of writing will be surprising to find if we think that spirituality must always be explicit. It may come as a surprise, for example, to discover that spirituality may be informed and nourished by reading novels. All the best novels address life's big questions and may be read through the lens of faith. We find ways to nourish our souls that suit our taste and probably gravitate towards tried and tested writers and genres, but it is hoped that this collection will give us the confidence to step outside those immediately trusted authors to see what someone from a different perspective has to say to us. We do not always have to agree with everything an author has ever written in order to benefit from her work. A challenge is as necessary for growth as a comforting affirmation.

I am aware that the collection is limited to western writers and would have liked to include voices from other parts of the world. In the end I was guided by the limitations of space, the need for coherence and ready access to the works of the writers included here. We need to hear voices from other parts of the globe, however, and to allow them to enrich and challenge our horizons.

The book does not set out to critique the writers included. I have not attempted to evaluate their works as literature, as the aim of the book is to appreciate the range of writing that addresses spirituality rather than literary criticism.

Women as writers

Do women write differently from men? Is there such a thing as 'women's spirituality'? These are important questions to bear in mind as each author is encountered. Who would be most likely to read *x* or *y*? Is a particular author a 'women's writer' only or would men benefit from reading her as well?

I did not set out to write a feminist critique of spirituality, or to advocate the separation of men and women where spirituality is concerned. Certainly it is the case that women once wrote under very different conditions from men. Think of the Brontë sisters, who had to change their names to masculine ones in order to be published. The majority of women were semi-literate for far longer than men, being able to read but not write. In 1949 Simone de Beauvoir described women as the second sex in her study of their status and self-image in history and exhorted them not to settle for being amateurs. Some, but not all, in this volume write for a living, and times have changed considerably since de Beauvoir wrote.

It is true to say that the Christian Church has not often led the way in championing women as human beings created equally with men in every respect, and only in 2019 are we celebrating 25 years of women priests in the Church of England, but the women presented here are full of the courage and determination de Beauvoir urged women to cultivate. I have not chosen them because they write about women's issues, though I have wondered whether some of them will appeal to women rather than both men and women because of their writing style as well as the content of their work. Listen to your own response as you read.

Reading for spiritual growth

What part does reading play in spiritual formation? For me, reading has always been a source of spiritual food. I have read to learn, and to feed my soul as well as my mind. Reading has comforted me in lonely and barren times, challenged me out of my complacency, strengthened me in uncertainty and helped me see clearly when life has been confusing. Reading has enlarged my world in so many ways.

We read books to nourish our capacity to think, to reason, to know, to discern, to remember. The best writing engages the whole of us: heart, mind, body and emotions in an integrated fashion. Books are savoured for many reasons, and the love of reading expands our sense of who we are. Reading can be approached in a variety of ways, including as an academic exercise, to glean information to help us explain and analyse. It can also be an exercise in pleasure and enjoyment. Then there is reading for formation, where it is devotional and instructive at one and the same time. There was a time when study and prayer were regarded as one and the same thing.

It is reading for enjoyment and formation that is being explored here in the main, although hopefully there is information to absorb as well. Through reading, we enter other worlds that illuminate our own. Reading words on the page instructs us in the task of reading the rest of life: the mood of a room full of people, the face of a stranger, the season of another's soul as they unburden themselves to us, the right time to do something new, and so on. Reading the signs of the times is a Christian imperative, easy to get wrong but vital to persist in doing. Reading words that convey ideas and facilitate conversation between people so that we continue to learn and grow is also an essential aspect of Christian faith. Writing in *The Word in the Wilderness* about when Dante first met Virgil at the beginning of the *Divine Comedy*, the poet Malcolm Guite comments:

> It may be that hidden in the poets and writers we love best is a vital clue about the heaven we are aiming for; that we should stay with and return often and with confidence to those lines and images that have most inspired us, even from our childhood.[6]

Sarah Clarkson's *Book Girl* brilliantly illustrates this.

All books are written from a particular point of view. They have always played a role in the way faith has been expressed and explored.

Good books should help us to live life more fully, and good Christian books should help us to love God more deeply. They do this by enlarging our vision.

I suspect that several of the writers here would prefer to leave the label 'Christian' aside, for this would be to make explicit what they regard as implicit and all pervasive. Some writers address Christian themes implicitly but rather as if they are weaving a tapestry, not attaching a veneer to a world where God is not already present.

Today, religious language has become derided as unbelievable, and for many it is alien and absent from their world, so we need to find ways to make Christian faith accessible and to explain what it is about. Poetry, especially, brings a freshness of expression and draws us to what lies beyond the words.[7]

On reading well

Recently there has been a renewal of interest in reading well, with a number of books about books and reading being published – for example, Michael McGirr, *Books that Saved my Life: Reading for wisdom, solace, and pleasure*; Tim Parks, *Pen in Hand: Reading, re-reading and other mysteries*; Karen Swallow Prior, *On Reading Well: Finding the good life through great books*; Anne Bogel, *I'd Rather Be Reading: The delights and dilemmas of the reading life*.

What does it mean to read well in our fast-paced, visual culture where we are exposed to information overload and encouraged to consume but not digest as much as we can take? Reading can be transformative, but it can also be hard work, for we have to get into the mind of the writer and understand where he or she is coming from. We will find some of the writers here speaking our language, as it were, while others will need extra effort to enter their world. We may need to work at the style, the language, the content in order to enter fully into the text. We are trying to see the world from another's point of view, and this demands effort, like all spiritual disciplines.

There are books we may struggle with and books we may wish would never end, so engrossing is the world they invite us to inhabit for a while.

Reading has always had the potential to revolutionize people's thinking on a grand scale. It has tremendous power to effect change and has been as much feared as exploited throughout history. The Church at the time of the Reformation, for example, burned at the stake writers of reformist tracts, translators of the Bible and printers of suspect texts. I have a book at home entitled *Women who Write are Dangerous*,[8] reminding us that women writers have a powerful instrument to hand in books.

A writer's life

W. H. Auden thought that the life of a writer was irrelevant to his or her work:

> A writer is a maker, not a man of action . . . no knowledge of the raw ingredients will explain the peculiar flavour of the verbal dishes he invites the public to taste: his private life is, or should be, of no concern to anybody except himself, his family and his friends.[9]

I beg to differ with Auden, for I have always found that to know something about the context and life of a writer is to understand better the questions he or she asks and the concerns that drive her or his writing. The first author I learned about was Charlotte Brontë whose novel, *Jane Eyre*, was one of the earliest 'grown-up' books I can remember reading. To read about her life with her sisters, brother and father at Haworth Parsonage made me return to the novel with fresh eyes. To understand the social background of Charlotte and the expectations of women, especially women writers, of the period, made *Jane Eyre* all the more essential reading in my eyes.

I have always wondered about the lives of the writers whose works I love, and I have enjoyed getting to know the authors chosen for this volume. I have met some of them but have had to rely on researching biographical details for most of them. Some are more well-known figures than others and there is information in the public domain. Some reveal a lot about themselves in their books, for their story is integral to what they choose to write about. Others are less well known and stay in the shadows as they write. With writers who dare to write about prayer and spirituality, it is surely important to know something of why they write as they do. A mother of a large family will write differently from a single woman committed to a life of celibacy in community, yet both have vital things to say to enhance our vision of the world. An urban saint will write about different subjects from someone living in a remote part of the countryside, and so on.

Reading and writing and the Christian faith

The authors featured in this volume write as members of a long tradition. Writing down their prayers has long been a practice for Christians, and others have used them and been blessed by them. The Christian tradition has valued books as a way to disseminate teaching and preserve learning. Christians have explored new ideas through books, engaging with culture and society, science and politics. They have encouraged believers in times of persecution and distress through literature of various kinds. Study, as we have seen, is one of the classical spiritual disciplines involving reading, writing and texts.

For many Christians, spiritual reading is a primary means of spiritual nourishment, but it demands a different approach. Reading slowly and meditatively the texts of spiritual classics connects us to the praying Church of the past and reminds us that we live in a community where faith has been handed on, often through books. There was a time, for example, when every home in England had a copy of John Bunyan's *Pilgrim's Progress* sitting alongside the Bible. There is a place for Christian paperbacks too, those books of the moment that speak into our own times, challenge us in our own context and tell of God at work in our own world. My childhood and teenage years fed on stories about missionaries and contemporary moves of the Spirit. I learned about how God took care of Corrie ten Boom in the death camps during the Second World War in *The Hiding Place* and I found encouragement as a shy student in books like Rebecca Manley Pippert's *Out of the Saltshaker and into the World*, in which I learned about the ways that Christian faith speaks into the culture of the day.

One of the most formative books in my early life was *Mary Jones and Her Bible* by Mary E. Ropes. I was deeply impressed that this young girl, aged 15, who had been taught to read by the travelling schools set up in Wales by Thomas Charles, walked barefoot for 26 miles in order to purchase her own copy of the Bible in Welsh. The privilege of the gift of reading has never left me. I have often given books as gifts because I believe they continue to have a vital role to play in spiritual growth.

It is good to know that the recent prediction that books would soon be history has not been realized and that in fact more people say that they much prefer a real book to an electronic version. While small bookshops continue to exist precariously, the sale of books in general is on the rise and many bookshops are thriving in new and exciting ways. Nevertheless, there is an element of fear around books and reading which needs to be acknowledged. Maybe memories of struggling at school, being told you are stupid by a teacher or growing up in a home where books were scorned, or all of these, has led to a distrust of books that goes very deep.

The Christian Church has a long and valuable heritage of reading and writing which could be open to many more people than those who believe they can access it at present. Whenever I visit a church I look to see if there is a bookstall. Sometimes there is a sad excuse for one, with a few dog-eared, out-of-date volumes lying on a dusty shelf, which makes me wonder when was the last time anyone recommended a good book in that church. It is sometimes argued that many people, especially younger people, still read, but are likely to turn to a blog or an online article rather than buy a book. It is not an either/or culture – or it need not be. This book is in part a way of encouraging more people, women and men, to take up a book and read.

While books about books are in fashion again, biographies of writers have never gone out of fashion. Books about women show no sign of disappearing, and recently there has been a plethora of books listing ten women who did x or y, or one hundred women who changed the world in this way or that, and various other collections of women whose names are deemed worthy of being remembered. This book is written to draw attention to good women writers who write on Christian themes in the hope that they will become better known and appreciated.

1

Kathleen Norris: everyday mysteries

Do you find that everyday tasks seem to get in the way of what you really want to be doing? I am thinking of things like the washing-up, contacting the car insurance firm, taking the cat to the vet and so on. If this sounds familiar, you have probably not connected this frustration with the book of Leviticus. Kathleen Norris does so with the following observation:

> The Bible is full of evidence that God's attention is indeed fixed on the little things . . . It is in the ordinary, the here-and-now, that God asks us to recognise that the creation is indeed refreshed like dew-laden grass that is 'renewed in the morning' (Psalm 90:5), or to put it in more personal and also theological terms, 'our inner nature is being renewed every day' (2 Corinthians 4:16). Seen in this light, what strikes many modern readers as the baffling attention to detail in the book of Leviticus, involving God in the minutiae of daily life – all the cooking and cleaning of a people's domestic life – might be revisited as the very love of God. A God who cares so much as to desire to be present to us in everything we do.[1]

Conflict of interests

Kathleen Norris, a poet as well as a prose writer, was born in Washington, DC, USA, in 1947 and had her first book of poems published when she was in her twenties (*Falling Off*, 1971). She had a Christian upbringing and a grandfather who was a preacher, but for a long time she believed that being a writer and being a Christian were incompatible.

I have met so many people who have believed that being a Christian would mean that any attachment to art, literature, music, or indeed any non-church-based passion, would have to be given up. Do you like running? It will get in the way of your commitment to Christ. Are you a gifted painter? What has that got to do with saving souls? This kind of dualism has infected Christian belief to the extent that Christians have sometimes abandoned the world outside the ghetto of the Church, which has led to the world inside being impoverished and grey.

The other symptom of such dualism is an anti-intellectual attitude both within and without Christian circles. In church circles it is often thought that too much knowledge leads to hubris and damage to belief. Beyond the Church it is often assumed that Christianity requires us to abandon the mind in order to believe. Influenced by the educational and psychological ideas of the 1950s and 1960s, which claimed that religion was something to grow out of, Kathleen thought that her poetic work would be diminished by believing. This led to a struggle which was not helped by the absence of good role models among her writing contemporaries. She eventually came back to faith, but returning to church after such a gap alerted her to the alienating nature of much of the churchy language she heard. Nevertheless, return to church she did.

Kathleen eventually served as a temporary pastor of Hope and Spencer Memorial Presbyterian Churches in Keldron and Lemmon, South Dakota. She has also taught writing classes to students and young people. For someone who values words and their power to express the inexpressible, at least in a small but significant way, Kathleen Norris has worked very hard to find ways in to the mystery that is God.

Influences

I discovered Kathleen Norris via the *Rule of St Benedict*, the ancient monastic document that became the foundation of the Benedictine order of monks and nuns that has been so formative in the history of the Christian Church. The desert and Benedictine traditions of spirituality have been vital to Kathleen's return to Christian faith, helping her to overcome hurdles to belief and practice. Having experienced the way that language can make us feel excluded and shut out, and that faith is inaccessible, Kathleen stumbled across a Benedictine monastery where she discovered worship that was far more accessible and refreshing to her:

> The monks, it seemed, were in less of a hurry, less frantic to fill the air with a quantity of words. They allowed for silence, room in which the words of Scripture and Christian theological tradition might more readily be taken in, digested, absorbed. Day in, day out, they immersed themselves in the poetry of the psalms.[2]

Speaking like a Christian

I warmed to Kathleen's honest, inquiring style of writing and went on to read her other books and found that they all have the same qualities of inquiry and insight. I return to her books when it feels as though church has grown stale or I recognize my need to earth my faith deeper in the real world. I especially appreciate the way she unpacks religious language to find everyday metaphors to help us understand the nature of God and Christian faith. She is interested in words, especially religious words.

Are there ways of talking about religious themes in everyday language that connects with people's lives and makes us thirst for more? Kathleen believes there are and seeks to strip away the religiosity of so much 'Christianese' as she writes. *Amazing Grace: A vocabulary of faith* is a kind of lexicon, compiled in the firm conviction that human beings are storytellers for whom understanding the dictionary definitions of religious words, while useful in understanding our religious heritage, is less important than the lived experience of them within that tradition. A good example is the word 'creed'. Kathleen compresses the wide range of Christian faith and belief into a few words which to many people can feel like a verbal straitjacket.

The Creeds were hammered out in the early centuries of the Church as it found it necessary to define itself over against those whose beliefs stretched its teachings too far one way or another. In one sense, the Creeds simply tell the story of salvation as understood by Christians: that Jesus came, died and rose and will come again; that the Holy Spirit who came at Pentecost also spoke through the prophets; that there is forgiveness of sins and the promise of eternal life. At their worst, the Creeds conjure up a shopping list of beliefs that people must comprehend and assent to before joining the Church. Kathleen wonders exactly how many people fully comprehend the meaning of the words in the Creeds: 'God of God, Light of Light, Very God of very God', for example.

Faith and doubts

Kathleen also relates how the fact that she had plenty of doubts herself did not stop her from attending church. She simply took them there with her.[3] This takes a good deal of courage. Most people assume that those already in church have overcome any doubts and are full of confidence in what the Church professes. This is unlikely to be the case. Many Christians do not admit to doubts for fear of being judged and found wanting. In some instances we fear to voice doubts even to ourselves lest the whole edifice of faith comes tumbling down. Who has never had a feeling of doubt about some aspect of Christian belief or the expectations laid on people by institutional religion?

Kathleen was helped by reading a Benedictine monk who wrote that the Semitic world of the Bible is a world where story carries more weight than doctrine and where a creed begins: 'A wandering Aramean was my father,' she says.[4] Another monk suggested to her that doubt is merely the seed of faith, a sign that faith is alive and ready to grow. Kathleen was surprised that the Benedictine monks did not seem at all fazed by her doubts. Indeed, they informed her that 'God can work with doubts'. It is a theme that Kathleen returns to in her writing a number of times, not only because it troubled her so much, but also because she understands how it plagues so many and gets in the way of practising faith. *Amazing Grace* is especially helpful in unpacking it.

It is often said that the opposite of doubt is not certainty but faith, and it is faith that Kathleen is interested in exploring. Although she struggled with doubts, especially when she was young, she discovered that faith itself was a powerful enough draw to enable her to overcome them over time. She realized that she did not have to understand everything before committing herself to faith.

When she returned to church in her thirties, however, she felt bombarded by the very vocabulary of the Christian faith. Words like 'blood', 'heresy', 'repentance' and 'salvation' seemed dauntingly abstract to her, even vaguely threatening.[5] She found that she needed to rebuild her religious vocabulary so that the words she could no longer take for granted, as she had done in childhood, could become real to her in an existential sense. This sounds highly relevant for the contemporary Church as a whole to hear today in a world that is profoundly disconnected from the culture of Christianity. The increasingly small minority who have been brought up in the Christian faith need to make that faith their own as they mature into adulthood or it will be vulnerable to fracture, while the institutional Church requires constant vigilance against assuming it is speaking in ways that people can hear in a post-Christian world.

Some have suggested that Christians should simply drop the difficult religious language and find alternatives. The result has sometimes been a watering down of profound truths and a language littered with the banal. Kathleen is more interested in unpacking the words and exploring what they might look like in ordinary, everyday terms. Like 'Love' in George Herbert's poem, *Amazing Grace* has a gentle approach, 'sweetly questioning' in order to draw us closer to God. The result is more of an invitation than a threat. Similarly, as a preacher in her church in Lemmon, Kathleen determined not to use religious words like 'sin', 'hell' and 'righteousness' without explaining them, so that her hearers could enter into a better understanding and find a way to inhabit them that made sense and helped them connect life and faith.

Spiritual geography

Besides the language we use to talk about God and faith, the question of what it all looks like in a life lived in this or that particular context is vital to our spiritual lives becoming authentic and practically possible. Geography is thus of great interest to Kathleen Norris, for she believes that the physical landscape has an impact on our spiritual life. Her book *Dakota: A spiritual geography* explores this theme. North and South Dakota are inhospitable regions of the USA, home to the dustbowls of the 1930s, and she writes sympathetically and with deep insight about the people who struggle to make a living on the Great Plains today.

The book is an extended metaphor about the spiritual life as it is lived in place and time. Growing up in a town or a village in a flat part of the world as opposed to a mountainous region, or in a country blessed with regular rainfall rather than the threat of drought for much of the time, has an influence on how we view the world. Kathleen argues that we do not take seriously enough the influences that life has on the shaping of us. Although we read of dust, wind and drought and the harsh beauty of the land, this is not a 'back to the land' book. It is a superb example of what is known as spiritual geography, the way that the physical landscape has an impact on human beings and contributes to spiritual formation. 'Dakota is a painful reminder of human limits, just as cities and shopping malls are attempts to deny them.'[6]

One of the key moments in Kathleen's life was when she inherited her grandparents' farm in Lemmon, South Dakota, in 1974. Here, in a small town of 1,600 inhabitants, Kathleen learned about encountering God in very ordinary circumstances and in the routine of daily life. We are shown how the Great Plains of South Dakota became the place where she encountered the sacred. She describes the silence and the enormous spaces in that 'land of little rain and few trees, dry summer winds and harsh winters, a land rich in grass and sky and surprises'.[7] It is a land of extremes, and the way they come together reflects the extremes we experience in the ordinary contradictions of human life.

Kathleen made a conscious choice to stay put, encouraged by the Benedictine value of stability, and thereby learned about inheritance, relationships, being countercultural, hope, humility and, in short, how to be a human being. She writes about the frontier and how the church for her became both a new and an old frontier. The frontier is the place where we build on the past for the sake of the future. Thinking about her own past, she reflects on her two grandmothers, both devout Christians but with very different spiritual outlooks, one being austere and fierce, the other more generous and open. Her reflections led me to think about those close to me in childhood who shaped my image of God through the way they expressed their faith.

Connecting with the sacred in life

For anyone hungry for a contemplative approach to life, Kathleen Norris offers ways to connect with the sacred in whatever landscape we find ourselves in. Likening the prairie to the ocean it once was, she notes that it helped her to realize how small and vulnerable human beings really are, and it taught her humility before the vastness and grandeur of God. This took her to Job 38, where God confronts Job with the majesty of the created world and asks him, 'Where were you when I laid the foundation of the earth?' (verse 4).

The sense of the sacred at the heart of her book, Kathleen argues, may be found anywhere. She found it on the great prairie, but it is just as present in towns and cities or whatever geographical location we inhabit, if only we can open our eyes to see. Kathleen uses the physical landscape as a metaphor for the monastic cell and the practice of prayer that satisfies the hunger for God. This kind of attention to where we live and spend our days has become increasingly important in a culture less and less connected with the natural world. Ironically, in a world governed by technology designed to help us connect, we are also less and less connected, at least physically, with one another.

Neither do we have the resources that a less-connected age offered. As a child I spent many hours outside by myself in ways that shaped me as I grew up. These included a large ash tree in the field next to our house, which had a swing underneath. I would sit there for hours sometimes, simply listening to the wind in the tree and enjoying the solitude. Though I did not think of it as a sacred place at the time, looking back it was deeply grace filled in the sense that Kathleen speaks about the Great Plains, for it was a place where I encountered something greater than myself and found comfort and perspective in my smallness and a sense of connectedness with the world around me.

Kathleen Norris and St Benedict's Rule

We learn more about the impression the Benedictine tradition made on Kathleen in *The Cloister Walk*, which describes in more detail how immersing herself in the life and rhythm of a Benedictine monastery was an important step in returning to church. The discipline of simply turning up to the regular practice of prayer in the monastery slowly seeped into her being and drew her in. Living alongside the monks for a time, Kathleen observed their life together and the importance of belonging to a community of faith.

Benedictine religious communities continue to follow the *Rule of St Benedict*, which Kathleen calls one of the most influential books of all time. The *Rule of St Benedict* was shaped by the spirituality of the desert in the fourth and fifth centuries, where Christianity flourished among the desert dwellers. Written by St Benedict of Nursia in the fifth century for the ordering of communal life among his fellow monks, the *Rule* is largely Scripture rearranged to set out a way of life and worship centred on Christ. How is it that an ancient text like this, written in a landscape so different from that of most people's experience, not only continues to shape the lives of so many Christians but also critiques our lifestyle and values in the modern sophisticated western world? Is it in part the fact that it is rooted in a way of understanding and appropriating Scripture? Kathleen points out that there would be very little left of the *Rule* if all the biblical references and quotations were to be removed.

Kathleen Norris returned to faith as a Protestant, but the riches of the Benedictine tradition go beyond denominational boundaries. In 1986 she became a Benedictine oblate, someone who remains lay and lives in the world but who follows as closely as possible the rhythms of prayer, work and study that lie at the heart of the Benedictine way of life. Her gratitude to the Benedictines is no personal infatuation on her part, for it is generally recognized that, next to the Bible, the *Rule* has shaped western culture from the early Middle Ages onwards. In *Amazing Grace*, she wrote,

> If, as I believe, God-Talk is a form of idolatry, a way of making
> God small and manageable, then God's presence in the

Benedictine rhythm of work and prayer is too large, too various, too unpredictable to be contained by it. The idolatry of God-talk, like all idolatry, is a symptom of our desire for control, and Benedictines admit too much of the Bible into their daily lives to keep God neatly packed into their comfort zones.[8]

An everyday God

Kathleen Norris is constantly cutting religiosity down to size. Her concern is to let God be God and to help us enlarge our expectations of the Lord's ways. The juxtaposition of the wonder of grace and the ordinary ways we encounter that God is key to her writing style. The way this always arises out of her own experience is an invitation to us to reflect on our own experiences and to discover the ways that God has been there all the time.

As someone who was brought up on stories of heroes of the faith who had dramatic conversions followed by amazing ministries, it has taken me many years to realize that there is nothing ordinary about ordinary, everyday life when it is viewed from the perspective of eternity. God is present as we change nappies, run domestic errands, care for an elderly relative or simply turn up for work each day. It's just that we fall for the fallacy that God is only interested in the 'holy', the explicitly Christian and the big moments of life. On the contrary, all of life is holy, and the life of faith is a daily commitment to following Jesus in every aspect of life, however hidden it may be.

Neither do we have to understand everything about faith intellectually in order to be a 'good' Christian. Kathleen describes the routine of simply 'showing up' to the daily offices, for example, as being part of how she found a meaningful Christian faith that did not rely wholly on intellectual comprehension. She writes about the role of repetition in developing faith that can endure.[9]

For anyone who is wondering whether it is worth continuing with spiritual practices that don't seem to yield much in the way of an imagined 'wow' factor, this is a great encouragement to persevere. One of her most helpful books about the ordinariness of life providing spiritual nourishment and insight is a brief work called *The Quotidian Mysteries*, tellingly subtitled: *Laundry, liturgy and 'women's work'*. (*The Quotidian Mysteries* is an extract from her full-length book, *The Noonday Demon* – see below.)

Spiritual lethargy

The recognition that so much of the practice of faith is routine and ordinary, yet precisely where God meets us with grace, is key to Kathleen Norris' spirituality. Much of her writing concerns reflections on ordinary life interspersed with autobiography, a feature of many of the authors included in this collection. She writes about routines, childhood memories and people who have been part of her story, and she is honest about her personal struggles with depression and caring for her husband in his illness. So much of this is small scale – the few who gather to worship in local congregations, rather than the big hyped-up worship event; the ordinary day-to-day business of living rather than the big moments of fame or success.

Kathleen was widowed in 2003 and wrote about caring for her husband in his illness in *The Noonday Demon*. The title of the book is a reference to its subject, *acedia*, a word difficult to translate exactly, but denoting a concept that was all too familiar to the desert Christians of the ancient world. It manifests itself as a lack of energy, focus and feeling, giving rise to a kind of listlessness. Once discussed alongside other key distractions from God, such as pride, sloth and greed, the formalizing of human sins led to its disappearance (the reasons for which are explored by Angela Tilby in *The Seven Deadly Sins*[10]). *Acedia* did not make it into the list of the seven deadly sins, yet it continues to worm its way into human lives, perhaps more than ever in the twenty-first century, where boredom and meaninglessness has strengthened its grip. A 'couldn't care less' attitude or the experience of feeling drained of energy as one day turns into another is familiar to many even in our frantic culture. It is the reason we are always looking for the next thing to stimulate and distract us.

The Noonday Demon contains Kathleen's reflections as she becomes a carer. It is infused, as always, with her keen interest in the early monastic tradition. It is subtitled *A modern woman's struggle with soul-weariness*, suggesting that this ancient affliction is highly relevant to our culture today. One of the interesting questions it raises is why *acedia* fell out of Christian consciousness and how it has continued to seduce people, never more so than in our contemporary world – it simply manifests itself in new guises. Kathleen's study of *acedia* is part diagnosis, part memoir and part spiritual meditation, resulting in a book that is both hopeful and unsettling at the same time.

In an interview for Homiletics Online, Kathleen commented, 'People hunger for stories, good language and books about serious things that aren't huge scholarly tomes that are hard to read.'[11] In fact, Kathleen knows a great deal about the early Church and its spiritual writers, but she wears her learning lightly. Quotations from these spiritual teachers and stories of the lives of the Desert Fathers and Mothers, along with references to Scripture, interweave with her own story to create a landscape in which readers can find many points of contact from which to explore their own experience.

Key themes

- Spiritual autobiography
- The influence of place on spirituality
- A Protestant appreciation of the *Rule of St Benedict*
- Finding God in the ordinary routines of life
- The language of faith
- Doubt and faith

Questions and action points

- Are there any religious words from sermons you have heard that you feel need reframing or explaining for today's hearers? How would you explain them?
- 'The ordinary activities I find most compatible with contemplation are walking, baking bread, and doing laundry.'[12] What ordinary activities help you connect with prayer?
- Are there any places that have provided you with a sense of the sacred? Where are they and what do they convey to you?
- How important is it to you to understand everything you believe? What parts of Christian teaching are you prepared to take on trust as mystery?
- Take a period of your life and write about it in connection with your journey of faith. What was happening? How would you describe it in terms of spiritual geography?
- Have you experienced *acedia* as described by Kathleen Norris? How did it feel and what helped you to persevere?
- Is there a historical spiritual tradition that has especially informed your understanding of Christian faith? What are its key features that draw you in?

Select writings

Amazing Grace: A vocabulary of faith (Oxford: Lion, 1998).

The Cloister Walk (London: Riverhead Books, 1996).

Dakota: A spiritual geography (New York: Ticknor and Fields, 1993).

The Quotidian Mysteries: Laundry, liturgy and 'women's work' (New Jersey: Paulist Press, 1998).

The Noonday Demon: A modern woman's struggle with soul-weariness (Oxford: Lion Hudson, 2008, 2009).

2

Alison Morgan:
following Jesus

Can you remember when you first felt an awareness of God? And
what about your first sense of being a Christian? We come to God
in all sorts of ways, but we are all called to be disciples, followers of
Jesus. In fact, discipleship is the essential component of Christian
spirituality and could justifiably be an alternative and even a more
biblical word to use for all that spirituality means.

But what exactly is a disciple? How do we know whether we are
disciples or not? I think people have many different ideas about what
a disciple actually is. Alison Morgan is determined to get the concept of being disciples of Jesus back into the centre of the Church's
life and purpose. She does this through her writings and through the
work of The Mathetes Trust (see p. 36) which she founded with her
husband Roger.

Passionate faith

The first thing that struck me about Alison Morgan's writing was
its passion. Alison has a message she believes is world-transforming
and writes to awaken her readers to its vitality and importance. She
has an arresting way of writing, using poetry that is well known and
vivid metaphors of her own to explore and explain the concepts she
wants us to grasp.

Spirituality is often seen as lightweight and lacking in academic
rigour. Indeed, when it is decoupled from Christian content, it becomes whatever you or I want it to be. Alison Morgan could have

pursued an academic career; instead she has brought academic thoroughness to writing material that is accessible. It is full of human stories that enable us to remember that we are part of something powerful and life changing.

The second thing that struck me about Alison's writing was that, as I began to read her books and checked out her web page, I discovered that she is a keen birdwatcher and has described aspects of faith from the perspective of the natural world, especially birds. Her web page has a section on ornithology. It is full of her beautiful photographs of birds, in particular the common crane, the great white egret and the curlew. She has been watching birds from an early age, and when she was 16 she trained as a licensed ringer. She speaks in schools around the country about birds and is involved in various conservation projects.

The third thing I was intrigued and drawn in by was the combination of clear Christian teaching, a love of poetry and a sympathy for the natural world. This is discipleship that is rounded, involving the whole of life, and it is attractive.

The fourth thing that caught my attention was that she had studied the thirteenth-century Italian poet, Dante, for her PhD. Alison is a scholar and an expert on the writings of Dante and has published a widely acclaimed study of his work: *Dante and the Medieval Other World*.[1] As I had been trying to read Dante's *Divine Comedy* and, like Alison, loved the medieval take on the world, I had to find out more about this writer who had so many wide-ranging interests, all held together by her Christian worldview. It is clear that her love for Jesus and her desire to share the good news about him both drives her work and holds her different areas of interest together.

God's story and our story

Alison is one of the writers I was able to meet and interview, but something I had already discovered meant that I felt I knew a little about her before we met, and that was the way she draws on her own life story in her books. Her personal testimony and how faith became real to her forms so much of her approach to Christian faith and how she presents it in her various books. It is clear that the direction of her life and writing stems from the way she became a Christian, for it was her own search for truth that led her to devote herself to finding out what really mattered. Truth and its application is the driving force of the passionate clarity that characterizes her writing.

She describes her search for truth in *The Wild Gospel*, the book which, incidentally, she regards as her own favourite, how she had created a life based on contingent truth and how it all fell apart as she watched her friend and director of studies die. She went in search of absolute truth instead, through philosophy, history and experience.

For me it has been like a pebble dropped into a pond: it lands, splash, in the centre, clear and visible, at the moment of first encounter with Jesus; and yet its arrival is a beginning, not an end, for from the point of impact spring concentric ripples which slowly move over the surface of the pond in ever increasing and interdependent circles. God is at the centre; but then it turns out that God is at the circumference also. So the truth starts with God and has to work its way out over the surface of the pond from God, only to find its destination is also God. From the moment of impact there begins a dialogue, a dialogue between you and God, a dialogue which never ends, a dialogue which if honestly conducted will spread out into all areas of your life, into your relationships, and ultimately into the world you inhabit. This dialogue takes place, as dialogues must, in words; and it reflects and repeats a process that began at the beginning of time with the creation of the world itself.[2]

So faith, believing in Jesus, is all encompassing. It is not simply a matter of intellectual assent, but a life-changing message. We too are called to be followers of Jesus. Alison elaborates:

This has enormous implications for us today. If the world was spoken by God, if Jesus was the word he spoke, and if the words that Jesus spoke are the truth, then it must surely follow that we, also spoken by God in the moment of our creation, spoken to by Jesus in the moment or moments of our conversion, and spoken to by the Spirit of truth who lives within us, we too must speak. What then are the words that we must speak?[3]

Faith and writing

When I asked Alison why she writes, she talked about finding a Bible in a bookshop in Blackheath at the age of 16 and reading those words from the first chapter of John's Gospel about the Word of life, Jesus. She explained how she wants to continue bringing words to life so that people may connect with life. She aims to write something that changes things, rather than offers comfort or interest. I was reminded of Kathleen Norris' words of how 'people hunger for stories, good language and books about serious things that aren't huge scholarly tomes that are hard to read'.[4] Alison Morgan's books would qualify here.

If I had to sum up Alison Morgan's focus in her work, it would be the twin themes of Word and Spirit. Her belief in the power of words to create and reflect reality and her heartfelt cry for the Church to wake up to the truth that sets people free lead to a confidence in the gospel that is often sadly lacking. Without these twin pieces of dynamite, spirituality becomes nothing more than a consumer add-on, ephemeral and empty of either meaning or substance. She takes theologians of the last century to task for dissecting the Bible and cutting it down to a size that can be analysed and reduced to isolated parts and then wondering why it seemed to lose its power.

Metaphors of faith

The Wild Gospel is not a how-to book. Alison says:

> My aim is rather to paint a picture of new possibilities, and invite you, the reader, to enter into it; to impart the confidence to undress the gospel from its dull, restricting clothes, and reclothe it in the eye-catching colours of its original garb.[5]

Alison's special gift in writing is to use metaphors and stories to bring her themes to life. Many of these are her own, and it is not surprising that she has a love of poetry that revels in metaphorical language. Sometimes the metaphors have been around a long time, but she takes them and applies them in new ways or expands them to press home the point she wants to make. In *The Wild Gospel*, for example, she takes the biblical metaphor of a wall to reimagine the way the gospel addresses us.[6]

Imagine an old wall of bricks and mortar lashed by hostile weather. Sometimes the bricks wear away and crumble while the mortar remains strong. At other times it is the mortar that is less resilient, and it gives way while the bricks themselves retain their shape and strength. Alison likens the world that Jesus entered to the former image. The people of first-century Palestine (as referred to in *The Wild Gospel*) were the weathered bricks of conflict and poverty, but while they were being ground down, the mortar of their social and religious traditions remained strong and felt constricting. In contrast, our own culture has almost lost the mortar that once held us together and the bricks, still sound but without any sense of cohesion, are in danger of falling into a heap that is no longer a wall. This describes so well the tension between individual and society and sets the scene for Alison to show how Jesus came to propose neither a programme of social reform nor a new religion, but to speak into the culture for the individual. The gospel is about a relationship with God, not a set of religious rules or a social revolution. Jesus ministered *into* the culture, *for* the individual.[7] If a culture is like a story (another metaphor), the gospel comes into a culture rather like the interruption of a fact into a story.

The book goes on to examine the encounters Jesus had with individuals in the Gospels and also his teaching, exploring how everything he said and did involved inviting people to embrace a completely different set of values to live by, based on relationship with him. Alison summarizes for us a wide range of scholarship on the New Testament (the bibliography at the end is extensive and a useful tool for further reading). She then has a chapter covering the broad sweep of Church history to show that, time after time, the Church failed to grasp what it was being called to be. Instead of challenging the surrounding culture and calling people to repentance and faith, the Church has often assimilated the culture and eventually been absorbed by it. Yet the Church has endured because, when the simple gospel is proclaimed and lived out in different ways according to the culture in which it finds itself, it has been able to show a different and a better way to live.

Faith and our culture

For anyone new to Christian faith, this book is a great way to learn about the way the gospel has adapted to be able to speak into different historical and cultural situations. Many key figures are mentioned and the impact of their response to Jesus' call to follow him described, and the point is made that so many of these characters were ordinary men and women who 'punctured the story' of their culture and showed a countercultural way to live.

The whole point of the book is to awaken the Church to rehabilitate the truth of the gospel by becoming more real ourselves in our living of it and to believe that in the gospel we have a tool that will set people free from the lies our culture has sold them. To do this we have to clothe the gospel in the language of the culture, focused into the assumptions of the culture and offered as an example to the culture. The book explores what our culture is built on, its values and assumptions and how inadequate these are for human wholeness and meaning. On a visit to Africa, where a very different culture confronts her, Alison sees the failures of our own materialistic society. She does not, however, exalt African culture as the only way to be, for it too has mortar that imprisons and dehumanizes people. Without the gospel, all human cultures are heading in the wrong direction.

Alison conveys the way that the good news of Jesus changes everything through stories of individuals and communities that have responded to it and experienced such changes themselves. The extracts here show Alison to be an energetic and enthusiastic writer. She challenges me to join in with this wonderful divine project of speaking the word of truth through the power of the Holy Spirit within. As she does, she also challenges the culture of the Christian Church in the West today. Her writing is a great antidote to the weariness of so much church life.

A church for our context

I have focused predominantly on *The Wild Gospel* because Alison herself prefers this book over all the rest and because it contains all her main themes. In *The Word on the Wind: Renewing confidence in the gospel*, Alison continues the story by asking how we may be the Church for our context together.[8] What is the task to which we are called? Describing a fast-changing world, Alison argues that the issues that are posing challenges to the Church now are greater than those at the time of the Reformation. It is almost as though the Church has forgotten the key to what it is about. She also examines what it is that holds people back from sharing the good news.

The Word on the Wind has questions at the end of each chapter which make it useful for group study, as well as for the individual reader. It has some great memorable images too. It opens with a description of Mediterranean plants in Alison's greenhouse in Northamptonshire failing to grow in the chilly summer and notes that it seems as though we are trying to live out and share a Mediterranean gospel in a Northamptonshire greenhouse.[9] She likens people to trees and the culture to the soil and sets out to examine both. Thus we have an analysis of both the personal and the environmental aspects of faith today. The book presents some of the problems we face today and the emptiness of the so-called solutions – shopping, success and so on – and claims we need a different story to tell. Alison argues that we have one: Jesus.

There are lots of personal stories in this book, as there are in *The Wild Gospel*. Especially noticeable are stories of miraculous healing. These find their place in the worldview that Alison Morgan is proposing. She addresses two basic questions: how do we know things and how do we make sense of them? Two possible approaches may be taken. The first is a faith-based worldview, whereby we know things through revelation and our job is not to create our own meaning but to discover it. This is the Hebrew approach found in the Bible. The other approach is the Greek one of speculative inquiry. The book offers relevant and up-to-date discussion of the current state of scientific knowledge and the questions it asks and cannot answer. It also reminds us just how mysterious our universe really is. It is thus a great introduction to some key thinkers in the realms of science and theology for new Christians who are wanting to know more about their faith and how it relates to the modern world. Scientists such as John Polkinghorne, John Lennox, James Lovelock, Francis Collins and others feature, as do theologians from the early Church Fathers to more recent characters such as Wolfhart Pannenberg, Paul Tillich and Stanley Hauerwas.

Alison describes a life-changing visit to sub-Saharan Africa in *The Wild Gospel*, and how the request for help to disciple Christians with very few resources available led to the start of 'Rooted in Jesus' in 2002. The Mathetes Trust, for which Alison works, operates according to a simple biblical pattern: 'Watch me,' then, 'Off you go in pairs, you have a go and we'll go through it when you get back,' and, 'I'm leaving now, but you are to keep on doing it and teach others to do it too – and you will find that I am still with you.'[10]

'The plural of disciple is Church', says Alison, and here is a simple but effective way to grow disciples that is rooted in the way Jesus did it and taught his first disciples to do it too. It is an interactive and practical programme designed to help ordinary people follow Jesus in all aspects of their lives.

Following Jesus together

Following Jesus, Alison's third major book, completes the trilogy by looking at what the Church is meant to be as a community of disciples following Jesus together. The word 'disciple' is used more than 250 times in the New Testament (depending on the translation used). The word 'Christian' is used just three times.

In 2011, the Diocese of Gloucester carried out a survey among its clergy, asking what they thought the most important elements of discipleship were. The majority selected Bible study followed by prayer as activities of disciples. There was no suggestion that being a disciple should involve any kind of ministry or lifestyle. In fact, personal morality and witness came very near the bottom of the list of descriptions of disciples.

The English word 'disciple' comes from the Latin *disco*, meaning 'I learn'. For most of us, learning means classrooms and college. Learning involves knowing things. It takes place in our heads. I should know, as I spend an awful lot of time in a classroom teaching people about stuff, things they need to know. Our students spend an awful lot of time worrying about essay marks and exams. The Church has put a great deal of time and effort into producing materials about discipleship in courses, study days and Bishop's Certificates and so on. But – and it's a big But – that wasn't how Jesus taught his first disciples. Nor does it necessarily produce people who are well equipped to live and share their faith in everyday life.

The New Testament was originally written in Greek, not Latin, and the Greek word for 'disciple' is *mathetes*. The meaning of this word is nearer to an apprentice than a learner in a classroom. It involves not just learning from a master, but also learning to become more like him or her. Jesus taught in an apprenticeship-like way, gathering a group of people to be with him and teaching them to do the things he did – how to live and how to serve. And then he told them to teach others how to do the same. In fact, we could say that Jesus not so much taught his disciples but trained them. Rather in the way he himself had been trained to be a carpenter, in fact. Jesus was like a master craftsman whom they were to follow and imitate. 'Watch me,' he said.

Later he sent them out in pairs to try to do what they had seen him doing, and then they went back and told him about it so that he could go through it with them. Then finally he left them, promising that the Holy Spirit would be with them always and telling them to keep doing what they had seen and learned from being with him.

The bottom line is that we do not become disciples by going on a study course but by making a whole life response to Jesus in every part of our lives. Now this is both scary and extremely liberating at the same time. It's scary because none of us is let off the hook by saying that we're not clever enough, good enough, confident enough or whatever excuse we might think up. It's freeing because being disciples is not about what we know, but about who we are becoming. Our task is to get out of our heads and into learning how to apply the words of what is in there to our daily lives. It's a lifelong task. It's about embodying the good news about Jesus.

There is more good news too. Jesus never meant us to be isolated disciples, struggling on our own to do what he did. He called a group of people to be with him. They were to learn in community. The original group included fishermen, a tax collector, a political activist and a group of women. There were differences in temperament and in age. They were tasked with learning together, learning to love one another, accepting one another as brothers and sisters, and learning not to compete with one another or to judge one another. They were to be like the branches of a single vine. That pattern continued in all the churches we read about in the New Testament.

A love of words

All writers use words and enjoy them, even when it feels as if it will never be possible to express what we want to say. Alison Morgan's love of words is almost palpable. She is clear that words matter because they both reflect reality and create it.

Alison regards reality as something spoken. The Bible presents God's words as the active agents of life itself. She also notes that language is what distinguishes us from the other animals and makes us uniquely human, and she poses the likelihood that this is because we are made in God's image. Language determines how we think. Many scientists, Richard Dawkins included, refer to the creation of the universe in terms of words. DNA, for example, is often referred to as an alphabet, a single 64-word code that has spelled life in all living things from the beginning. It is the ultimate way of storing information. Physics comes down to information. But energy, too, is fundamental to everything that exists. Energy, power and life are all properties of the Spirit of God. They are evident throughout Scripture and are now available to us through the death and resurrection of Jesus.

Words begin in the imagination, and every reader should note carefully that Alison Morgan is writing about the truth of the gospel – the fact that punctures the story and the imagination that touches the heart and emotions. It has been said that nothing can be done that has not first been imagined. That is heartening for the artists and poets to hear, but we all need to hear this and exercise our imaginations much, much more. For anyone who thinks the Bible closes down our imaginations, Alison has a clear message:

> From Genesis to Revelation the Bible bears witness to the power of the imagination. God thought the world before he created it; he has already re-thought it and promised that he will therefore in the fullness of time re-create it.[11]

Meanwhile, we need dreams and visions that enable us to engage with our culture in creative and winsome ways to share the good news of Jesus. It is encouraging to see someone celebrating the great riches of being alive in order to do this. It is no surprise that Alison has published two anthologies of poetry that cover a great range of poets, well known and unknown. She often quotes poets in her writing to great effect, especially when they use an image that conveys something that catches the imagination. My favourite quotation is from Sir Thomas Browne, a seventeenth-century polymath who wrote about the Spirit that 'brooded on the waters and in six days hatched the world'.[12]

Learning from the birds

A good example of Alison's imagination and the way it informs her spirituality is in an article on birds and the spiritual life written for *ReSource* magazine entitled 'A Bird's Eye View'.[13] Weaving her own story with observations on birds and their habits, she encourages the reader to see them as signs of the reality and grandeur of God, but also as models of how we should be. Drawing on biblical material and writers from Church history, in her usual way, she argues that there is an affinity between the created world we can see and the spiritual world that we can't. She describes caring for a baby blue tit as an example of the latter. Outlining the routine of the baby bird each morning, she notes that he would get up, eat three mealworms, have a bath and then sit on Alison's finger and carefully preen all his feathers. This process was not all that impressive for he had not been taught how to do it by his bird parents. Then he would stand on one leg and sing.

Alison then describes how she takes time each morning to 'attend to the feathers' of her own soul. She runs her mind over each, smoothing, repairing, unfurling, fitting them for the day ahead. Her efforts are often not that impressive either:

Some of my emotional and spiritual feathers hang loose, and others are just growing, still in their waxy sheaths. I don't always manage to smooth them into place. But usually I too can sing, as I think of the God who made me and made the world, who gives me life and offers it to me anew each morning.[14]

To my delight, in this piece Alison quotes Anselm's advice to someone wanting to pray. The three photographs, which include one of Guy, the baby blue tit, were taken by her too.

Alison Morgan has written a number of shorter pieces which address important questions that Christians ask, such as *Renewal: What it is and what it is for.* She has written about healing in a practical training course, about the gifts of the Spirit and about dying. Christians have vital truths to speak of, though often don't know how to do so. In *The Word of God: What does it mean?* I was delighted to see that Alison quotes Annie Dillard on God thinking the universe.[15]

A section of her website entitled 'Summaries of useful books' lists numerous books under different categories, and clicking on them brings up notes made by Alison to guide the reader through the main points of the book.[16] Hopefully her notes make you want to read the whole book rather than settle for her take on each one. Categories include science and faith, prayer and the spiritual life, ministry in the context of our culture, renewal of the Church for mission, and ministry in Africa. There is a page with resources for prayer and reflection which also includes poetry collections compiled by Alison, with some of her own poems as well as other well-known authors.

Key themes

- The power of words
- The relationship between Word and Spirit
- The impact of Jesus
- Discipleship
- Being Church in context
- Apologetics

Questions and action points

- What part do Word and Spirit play in your spirituality?
- 'The truth starts with God.' Is this the case in your journey of faith so far?
- Alison aims to help her readers 'reclothe [the gospel] in the eye-catching colours of its original garb'.[17] Do you feel that this is a necessary thing for today's Church to seek to do? Why?
- Do you have a hobby or activity you enjoy that reminds you of faith in God? How does it do so?
- Alison believes in the power of words. How carefully do you choose what words to use? Has reading about Alison Morgan and Kathleen Norris in the previous chapter challenged you to pay more attention to words and how they are used?
- 'The plural of disciple is Church.' Do you agree? How closely does Alison's account of what the Church is for relate to your own experience?
- Alison uses vivid metaphors to unpack what she wants to say. Which ones have struck you most powerfully, and why?

Select writings

Dante and the Medieval Other World (Cambridge: Cambridge University Press, 2007, first published 1990).

Distilling Life, with Martin Cavender (eds) (Searcy: ReSource, 2012).

Doing What Jesus Did: A fresh look at the gifts of the Spirit (Searcy: ReSource, 2009).

Following Jesus: The plural of disciple is Church (Searcy: ReSource, 2015).

Renewal: What is it and what is it for? (Cambridge: Grove Books, 2006).

'Rooted in Jesus' (Somerset: Mathetes Trust) (also see <www.rootedinjesus.net>).

Something Understood (Somerset: Mathetes Trust, 2017).

What Happens When We Die? (Eastbourne: Kingsway, 1995).

The Wild Gospel: Bringing truth to life (Oxford: Monarch, 2004).
The Word of God: What does it mean? (Searcy: ReSource, 2008).
The Word on the Wind: Renewing confidence in the gospel (Oxford: Monarch, 2011).

Websites

<www.alisonmorgan.co.uk>
<www.rootedinjesus.net>

3

Ann Lewin:
watching for the kingfisher

Prayer is like _____. Perhaps you would like to fill in the blank. Countless books have been written about prayer, trying to describe it, explain it, understand it and help us to do it. Some attempt to simplify it; others seem to complicate it unnecessarily. In her poem 'Disclosure', Ann Lewin uses an arresting image drawn from the natural world that captures both its mystery and its power to draw us in.

She writes about similarities between prayer and birdwatching, specifically watching for the kingfisher. As with all birdwatching, we have to be in the right place – it's no good looking for sea eagles in your back garden, for example. And for prayer we need to find a place conducive to praying. Then we have to practise patience.

God, like the kingfisher, is not at our beck and call. We can't predict what he will do. God is consistent, like the birds in their behaviour, but, paradoxically, God is also unpredictable, mysterious and free.

The wonderful thing about Ann's poem is the way she concludes with a comment that reminds us how God encourages us in unexpected ways, just as the flash of blue indicates that the kingfisher is worth the waiting and watching.[1]

Ann says that poetry is a way of opening things up. Echoing Canon Mark Oakley, she reckons that if we change the full stops into commas, we open up words to provide spaces, into which we may enter and see afresh.[2] She called her first published poems *Unfinished Sentences* and insists that, really, she is a writer rather than a poet.

For some people, poetry must rhyme, even though most contemporary poetry does not do so. For others, there must be a definite rhythm along classical poetical lines. If you have a copy of the poem 'Disclosure', read it again and pause to notice when a word or phrase reminds you of something connected with your own praying.

Prayer and birdwatching

As we have seen with Alison Morgan, Ann Lewin is not the only writer in this volume to notice a link between spirituality and birdwatching. In linking prayer with birdwatching in a beautiful, poetic way, Ann has caught the imagination of Christians today who struggle to articulate what constitutes prayer and praying.

We live in an age that relies on experience and instantaneous gratification. The expectation, therefore, is that prayer should be uplifting every time. In the world of the immediate, we imagine that God will give us warm, positive feelings every time we seek his presence, and the absence of a felt confirmation of his love means there is something wrong. The truth of the matter is that we are called into a relationship with God that is nourished by prayer and needs to be regular and sustained, whether or not it delivers good feelings.

Much of prayer is mundane, 'just turning up', to quote Woody Allen. Like birdwatching, we do it even when nothing very much happens and there don't appear to be any signs that he is even listening. We do it, in other words, out of obedience rather than the desire for personal satisfaction. Prayer expresses our desire for God, and we have to concede that we are not in control. God will be God.

There is encouragement, too, in this poem. He has been there before, we are in the right place, and so we keep going in faith and trust that he could come again at any moment. The things we experience, such as a sense of space and expectancy, have benefits of their own to give us. They keep us grounded, facing in the right direction, in the right frame of mind. The whole point of the exercise, however, is that obedient attention to prayer is a preparation. It opens us up to be ready to receive. And sometimes, always at God's behest, we know for sure that he is present because a momentary revelation assures us and we are encouraged.

I experienced something like this which led me to awe, praise and thanksgiving only recently. Our friend had made an owl box and put it in his barn. Now, two years on, four owlets were ready to leave the nest. We settled down to wait, confident that they were in the box and must surely come out soon. Sure enough they did, and provided a wonderful cabaret as they practised flying in and out and learning to use their acute hearing skills. We were overawed by their silent beauty. The next evening we gathered to wait and watch again, but the weather was unkind and they did not show. We gave up eventually, disappointed but confident that they had been before and must surely come again. And they did, the same as before yet different, and reduced us to wonder. How Elijah on the mountain must have wondered what was happening when God did not show up in the earthquake, wind or fire as he had in times past. How surprised Elijah was by the 'sound of sheer silence' (1 Kings 19.12), and how the encounter changed him.

Noticing things

Like birds, God is always around somewhere, even when we are not especially looking. Different types of birds like different habitats – puffins like the sea, wrens like hedgerows and ditches, owls like the dark. God's habitat is everywhere and therefore he may turn up in the most unexpected places. Being prepared means we are more likely to notice the signs of his presence.

Ann's love of birds has fostered her ability to be still and to notice what is going on. She contrasts birdwatchers with twitchers, the latter being more interested in notching up another sighting on their ever-growing list of birds seen but not noticed. Twitchers are always in a hurry, rushing on to the next assignment, competitive and focused on achieving. They will never see the detail of a bird's plumage, learn its habits or bother to wonder.

Refusing to invest prayer with patient watching and waiting turns us into spiritual twitchers, leaving us dissatisfied and missing the point. Praying like a twitcher will mean we always pray in the moment, which is fine at one level but leaves no room for preparing our hearts to be open to receive. It will also carry a sense of breathless rush, rather than being held in the presence of the living God.

Crafting words

Ann Lewin has always been interested in words. Her vocation was to be a teacher, and teaching Religious Education and later English as well enabled her to fulfil her sense of calling. She has taught in comfortable schools and challenging ones and never wavered from her intention of encouraging others to rejoice in the power of words. She would give the children exercises that were similar to writing poetry.

Ann herself attended a convent school where the teachers were nuns. She recalls taking advanced English and a nun coming to read with them. This teacher always had a book with her so that she could read when there was a hiatus.

Reading, observing and writing are key to the creative process of working with words. Ann is clear about her lifelong calling, just as she is clear that she prefers to be called a writer rather than a poet. She writes free verse so regards her work as more like reflections than poetry. Their purpose is to help others see what is going on in their lives, to make connections and to be encouraged.

Ann says that she has always written, and looks back on a life where God has always been present: 'God got hold of me and has never let go.'[3] She began to attend evensong with her parents at the age of three because the Second World War meant that the service was moved to daylight hours to avoid problems caused by the general blackout rule.

For many years, Ann did not share her writing with anyone other than her spiritual director. It might have stayed that way except that writing about her own life coincided with the onset of her mother's dementia. Sharing her reflections on the experience of caring led to her publishing her own work for the first time. She was amazed by the response, for more than two thousand copies were either sold or given away, an indication that one person's experience can be of vital help to another.

What makes a poet or a writer? All of us have influences in our lives that shape our outlook, as well as, for some, clear determining events or people who have made us who we are. For Ann, Christian faith is foundational, and words filtered through liturgy and the Bible have been heard in a certain way throughout her life. When I asked her whether there have been particular poets who have influenced her, she mentioned a few classic names such as George Herbert, R. S. Thomas and Elizabeth Jennings. I noticed many others on her bookshelves: John Betjeman, John Donne and Malcolm Guite, for example. Reading poetry is one way of being inspired to try writing our own.

Exploring prayer led Ann to write about it; watching birds enlarged her capacity for contemplation, a stance that is vital for words to form within and to find expression on the page. She used to sit with her mother, a farmer's daughter, in the garden at home and listen to her talk about birds. Later she lodged with a keen birdwatcher who taught her a lot more. Life's experiences have also influenced her writing, especially the more difficult times. She understands that so much comes out of pain that has the potential for growth. Death, for example, so much a taboo subject still in our culture, needs to be brought into the open and to be talked about. Of course, this has been a fertile area for writing and has borne fruit such as liturgies and poetic reflections. Once asked to write an article with the title 'Creative joy', she agreed as long as a question mark was placed after 'joy'.

In one poem she writes about the sense of living on the edge of a map, which leads to hints of what is there, but no real clarity. She reflects that, had she been able to see clearly, she might have chosen a different route, cutting out the pain, perhaps, but also missing the breathtaking beauty. This mix of sorrow and joy, struggle and ease, are fundamental to what it means to be human, and a poem may capture this as nothing else can.[4]

A long tradition

Christian tradition has also played a part in shaping Ann's spirituality. The Benedictine tradition in particular lies at the heart of her approach, with its emphasis on the balance and interaction of prayer, rest and work (see the chapters on Kathleen Norris and Benedicta Ward for more on this theme). She has observed and been closely involved with the sufferings of other people, and has also experienced a good deal herself through personal illness and caring for family members in extreme circumstances. The Christian tradition has been a source of strength and has provided material for her own prayers and meditations as it has for so many down the centuries.

Ann has been especially drawn to Julian of Norwich, a female mystic and spiritual guide to many, who lived in the fourteenth century. She was also a writer, and the first woman to produce a book in the English language, called *Revelations of Divine Love*. It was written in 1393 when she was 30 years old. For centuries her work lay forgotten in a few monastic libraries until it was rediscovered and published for a wider audience at the beginning of the twentieth century. Since then, Julian and her writing have become well known both because of the theological and spiritual issues she addresses and the way she addresses them. She is sometimes referred to as 'a woman of our day'.[5]

During a life-threatening illness, Julian had a series of visions which she wrote down and spent the rest of her life reflecting upon. Her visions led her to reflect on God's nature and his attitude towards human beings. They raised questions of suffering, how to pray and how to face an uncertain future. Her great desire was that those who read her writings would be led to love God more through the assurance that they are beloved beyond all imagining.

That Julian is as relevant now as she was in her own time is of little doubt, despite the fact she was largely unknown for so long. Ann's deceptively simple book on Julian, *Love Is the Meaning*, brings her continued relevance to our attention in three main ways. First, she allows Julian to speak for herself with carefully chosen quotations. Second, she addresses the same questions that challenge us today as they did Julian and takes them seriously. Third, she uses her own material – poems, prayers and liturgical responses – to encourage reflection. In the chapter on sin, for example, she quotes Julian to show that Julian took sin very seriously and wrestled with its consequences and God's response. She talked to God in prayer and understood God to be showing her that Adam's sin was 'the greatest harm ever done or ever to be done until the end of the world'. In spite of this, however, nothing can stop God loving us, a point reiterated by Ann in her writing also.[6]

One of the reasons people are drawn to Julian is that she addresses God as mother. This, of course, is also why some people regard her with deep suspicion! Julian has been hijacked by feminists and heresy hunters alike. What she suggested, however, was rather different:

As truly as God is our Father, so truly is God our Mother, and he revealed that in everything, and especially in these sweet words where he says: I am he, that is to say: I am he, the power and goodness of fatherhood; I am he, the wisdom and lovingness of motherhood; I am he, the light and the grace which is all blessed love; I am he, the Trinity; I am he, the unity; I am he, the great supreme goodness of every kind of thing; I am he who makes you to love; I am he who makes you to long; I am he, the endless fulfilling of all true desires.[7]

Ann stays with the real Julian, noting that she did not substitute 'mother' for other images of God. She wrote consistently about God as Trinity and taught that God is always greater than anything we can imagine, more than any single image can convey. God also taught her that she 'should contemplate the glorious atonement, for this atoning is more pleasing to the blessed divinity and more honourable for man's salvation than ever Adam's sin was harmful'.[8]

Ann followed this up with a poem of her own that speaks of the power of the cross to atone for all our sins – our petty faults and failures as well as the headline-hitting atrocities. 'For my salvation' focuses on Jesus' bloodied knees, small wounds in comparison with his bleeding side and thorn-crowned head, but a reminder that my sins contributed to causing him to fall to his knees with the weight of them all.[9]

Ann goes on to stress the importance of being set free through forgiveness rather than constantly being weighed down by our sinfulness. We do this not by looking at ourselves but by contemplating God's mercy. She ends with the lovely image of parents who, when asked about their children, normally talk about them with love and pride in their development rather than launching into their faults and failings. If that is how earthly parents behave, how much more God?

For every season

In *Seasons of Grace: Inspirational resources for the Christian year*, Ann provides material for events in the calendar and moments that touch human life. The material is arranged in sections: Advent to

Candlemas, Lent to Pentecost and Ordinary Time. Each section begins with an introduction to the season and includes prayers, materials to help others pray and focus on Scripture, and suggestions for talks.

There are a number of brief essays on things such as the turn of the year, suffering and death, which face the big issues head on with an honesty that is straightforward and reassuring. These writings are simple but far from simplistic. They help Christians to link their lives with the Church's year and invite us to pause and live more deeply through the connection. As someone who enjoys making bread, for example, I could resonate with the chapter on Lammas Day, the beginning of August when a loaf baked with flour from the newly harvested corn would be brought into church and blessed. Reflecting on the old name for yeast, 'goddisgoode' (written as one word as if it were God's email, notes Ann), she comments:

> God is good. World events and the circumstances of our lives will knock that truth about, knock it down as dough is knocked down. But God's goodness is irrepressible, and the warmth of our response will help people to know the goodness of God.[10]

The same book offers resources to people who need help leading quiet days or worship events.

Perhaps as you read poems such as 'Ashing' and 'Candlemas Prayer' you will be inspired to seek out other poems related to the seasons, or even try writing your own prayer-poem.

In similar vein, by her gift of helping us to see God in the ordinary, Ann helps us to connect not only with the great feasts of the Christian year, but also with the lesser known and neglected moments. It is all designed to help us enter the story of faith ourselves, rather than viewing it from afar in ways that don't connect with our own experience. Ann is especially good at helping us see ourselves in the story, pointing out that stories necessarily involve us by their very nature. We use stories to discover our roots, to fire up our imaginations, to provide us with a vocabulary with which to talk about our own ideas and experience, to provoke us into a response and to remind us that we are not alone.[11] They 'give us back to ourselves with deeper understanding, seeing more clearly where our responsibility lies, which in turn frees us from the guilt which so often prevents us from moving on in our lives'.[12] With all this in mind, she turns to the Bible, which is full of stories that 'all contribute to one big story, the story of God's love affair with his people'.[13]

Although Ann is clear that our own imaginations are gifts from God, she offers ways in this book to help us get started, with resources for those looking for help in leading quiet days or worship events, for example. Ann is a writer who wants to serve others through her work, as do all the writers represented in this collection. Her writing is particularly practical but not prescriptive. It is more creative than that, and in turn aims to inspire creativity in the user.

Key themes

- Poetry and prayer
- The natural world as spiritual teacher
- Julian of Norwich
- Images of God
- Grief and loss
- The seasons

Questions and action points

- If you have a Bible that you read regularly, whether online or in paper form, how is it set out on the page? Does it, for example, have spaces around it, like a poem on the page? If you find yourself overwhelmed by words or come to passages of Scripture that are so familiar you cannot envisage seeing anything new, try reading from a Bible that has the text laid out as poetry when it is meant to be read as such and see if the spaces around the words encourage space in your head for reflection.

- Ann Lewin draws many parallels between prayer and bird-watching. Is there an activity that you enjoy or do habitually that reminds you of aspects of your relationship with God?

- In Chapter 2 of *Love Is the Meaning*, Ann reflects on imagery we use for God. She concludes the chapter with the comment, 'Julian's words can encourage us to be more adventurous in the language and imagery we employ when we think or talk about God.'[14] How do you react to the image of God as mother? Have you ever prayed to God as mother?

- All images of God are limited. For some of us, certain images – father and mother included – are problematic. Reflect on the qualities that both these images conjure up for you. How do they expand or challenge your ideas about God and God's character?

- Ann's experience of suffering and caring for close members of her family as they drew near to death has led her to comment that we do not talk about death enough. The last chapter of *Love Is the Meaning*, titled 'All shall be well', is about hope, yet its focus is pain and suffering. Ann asks readers what the challenges are that face us in learning to trust God in the face of suffering and death. She also asks what it means to regard God, as Julian did, as a vulnerable God. How might the answer to the second question shed light on the first?

- What are some of your favourite Bible stories? How have they connected with your own journey of faith?

Select writings

Come Emmanuel: Approaching Advent, living with Christmas (Norwich: Canterbury Press, 2012).

Love Is the Meaning: Growing in faith with Julian of Norwich (Norwich: Canterbury Press, 2006).

Seasons of Grace: Inspirational resources for the Christian year (Norwich: Canterbury Press, 2011).

Watching for the Kingfisher: Poems and prayers (Norwich: Canterbury Press, 2004).

4

Sarah Clarkson: for the love of books

I often find myself wondering which of the precious books on my shelves I would choose if I were told I had to let them all go apart from 40. Some volumes hold memories going back to childhood, some have been wake-up calls to do something different, some are oases of wisdom that I keep returning to for solace and strength.

Many writers trace their love of writing to books that are like friends pointing them towards the things that give life and direction. Sarah Clarkson is a good example of someone whose whole life has been shaped by books, which from an early age set her on the road to becoming a writer. She recognized the gift that reading is with an epiphany moment as a young adult and not only developed the sense of being formed by books, but also felt a compulsion to pass the gift on. She has written a guide to children's reading, *Read for the Heart*, for her own passion was first incited by her parents when she was a child.

How good books shape us

Sarah was brought up in a home crammed with books that had been gathered lovingly by her missionary parents, who were both writers themselves. Her earliest memories are of Vienna, although the family moved 12 times before she was 18. Books thus became a rock of stability amid constant change.

Living in that cultured environment, Sarah's parents recognized how important books are to a child, along with music and conversation. As well as encouragement from her family, Sarah had a mentor for a year, an anthologist who wrote to her and suggested books for her to read. He also taught her how to read, which may seem strange, but how we read matters as much as what we read.

Through reading, Sarah had a renewed sense of herself as an agent with power to learn, to discern, to grow and to create. This sense of agency is something that comes through with all of the writers represented in this collection. They want to help shape the world and are aware of the power of words to form their own lives, and then, as writers, they may be instrumental in shaping others.

How do we articulate the truth we discover both in those epiphany moments and in the ordinariness of everyday life? However much help writers have, in the end they have to find their own voice, and Sarah did so through blogging and writing her journal. Many of the writers in this volume found their voices long before the invention of the internet, but, as all writers discover, along with finding what to say, there is always the search for how to say it, closely followed by the question of how what we say will be heard.

Sarah Clarkson weaves something of her own story in and out of her writing, so it is always personal. A blog has an intimacy born out of immediacy that a book cannot have, but both media are flung out there to be placed at the mercy of the reader. This is not the place to debate the relative value of books and blogs and I am not a blogger, but Sarah is a writer who can handle both media competently, and books feature prominently as subject matter in both. Her most recent book is called *Book Girl* and is subtitled *A journey through the treasures and transforming power of a reading life*.

What makes a 'book girl'?

The big idea behind the book is that books not only help us to appreciate the wonder that is the world we live in, but they also shape us with their stories and thus enable us to live our own story within the world. In *Book Girl*, Sarah tells her story through the reading she has done at different stages of her life. C. S. Lewis wrote about that discovery of 'What, you too?' that is so enthralling when we discover that someone has experienced the same feelings in reading a book as ourselves.[1] Reading Sarah Clarkson's lists of books awakens that 'What, you too?' sensation time after time. I say this as an English girl reading mostly English books when growing up, and Sarah is an American girl raised on North American books. I have not read L. M. Montgomery's *Anne of Green Gables* (to Sarah's amazement), which was so influential on Sarah, but that only makes the sense of recognition all the more fascinating.

Books can divide, but they more often bring people together, and Sarah's book does more of the latter than the former. Indeed, when I read her four lists of 'books for growing book girls' there was only one section whose titles left me baffled (those recommended for girls aged between 8 and 13).

Good books cross great divides and facilitate a common sense of heritage. Sarah is convinced that reading books strengthens faith, and she aims to help her readers cultivate a love of reading for themselves. There are numerous annotated reading lists in her book so that readers can see at a glance what a particular volume is about. There are plenty of classics and plenty of books from secular contexts as well as explicitly Christian books. This is how it should be in our reading if we are to deepen our vision of the world and our place in it. I doubt there are many books that recommend *The Wolves of Willoughby Chase* by Joan Aiken and *Imaginative Apologetics: Theology, philosophy and the Catholic tradition* edited by Andrew Davison in the same volume.

I love the honesty of *Book Girl*, the way Sarah writes about her own vulnerability, how she can confess to disliking aspects of the books she recommends, how she leaves certain questions open ended, inviting us to read and make up our own minds. *Book Girl* aims to help anyone unused to reading to get started. It offers guidance on how to begin to form a reading habit, how to choose good books and what to look for in a book. It has themed chapters for different seasons of life, offering rich pickings for experienced readers and novices alike. These include books that stir us to action, books that fire the imagination, books to foster community, books that deepen the soul and so on. Some authors naturally belong in more than one category and we will no doubt see favourites as well as authors we have never heard of or considered before. Some of the chapters address explicitly Christian themes: prayer, the liturgical tradition of the Church, coping with brokenness and the need for hope. They offer new ways in as well as reminding us of old favourites that we might return to for further reflection.

On reading books about books

The temptation of *Book Girl* might be to be content to have read it, without picking up any of the books mentioned in its pages. Like prayer, it's easier to read about it than it is to get down to praying, and so it is with reading about books rather than reading the books themselves. Sarah's enthusiasm and carefully selected descriptions of individual books makes this less likely, however, especially if we utilize the categories in each chapter. Knowing where to go if in the future we feel in need of courage, for example, means that it is a book to keep on the shelf as a reference guide.

While it is always interesting to see the latest books that roll off the press, to have one recommended by another reader is at least as reliable as the effusive cover notes on many new books. I admit to reading a lot of book reviews in the knowledge that I have no hope of reading the whole book. There are books in Sarah Clarkson's collections that I will probably not get round to reading, but there are plenty with a 'x' beside them to make sure I do read them one day, simply because a single sentence has awakened my desire to read for myself. There is also the shared joy of seeing titles that I have read and loved and of pondering what someone else discovered in her reading of the text. The fact that reading fosters community is another theme of Sarah's book that hails from a family of readers who draw others in to share their insights.

Choosing what to read is a first step, but many of us need some help to read well. This process does not concern the business of learning the basics of literacy but that of seeing what underlies a book, its worldview, what the author is trying to do through the work, what messages are being conveyed and so on. The essence of reading well is paying attention, a theme that recurs in the writings of the women in this book. There are books that explicitly aim to train readers to read well, described in the chapter 'Books that talk back: My favourite books about books'.

Sarah is a powerful ally in my argument that anyone seeking spiritual insight should read novels, as they will find as much theology between their covers as in most theological tomes. Sarah could not help finding multiple connections between fairy tales and biblical narrative, doctrine and Victorian novels. She addresses the question that bothers some Christians more than others, which is what is acceptable for Christians to read and what is not? By emphasizing the importance of reading widely, are we saying read anything you like, only read so-called 'Christian books' or something in between? Sarah takes a different and much more wholesome approach by pointing out that if we are exposed to what is true, beautiful and good, we need not fear the dark side of life.

We need wisdom to navigate life, and practising discernment in reading is a good way to become more proficient at this. We do not need to filter out worldviews that differ from our own as long as we have learned to recognize them and understand what they are communicating. Thinking along the lines of 'How does a Christian worldview critique this?' (and vice versa, of course), rather than worrying about how many times it mentions God or Jesus, is a mature way to approach books and indeed much of daily life. The question that directs Sarah's own process of discernment is, 'What is it I hope to become?'

In a way, reading for spiritual nourishment is a bit like an apprenticeship. We read good books to glean wisdom for living and food for the soul, then we go and get on with living ourselves. We return to the books – at least, to the best of them – for encouragement and confirmation. Maybe some of us, like Sarah herself, find courage to practise the craft of writing too and so pass on this vital tool for spiritual nourishment.

Where does truth lie?

One chapter of *Book Girl* looks at the dichotomy some find in sorting fact from fiction in what we read. What is truth? Sarah admits that there have been times in her life when fictional stories helped to keep her believing more than anything else. Imagination, poetry, story and fiction are not mere decoration where truth is concerned, but are central to how we understand what truth is. Faith is not a series of facts to be believed and certainly cannot be 'proved' in a scientific way. We need allegory, metaphor, imaginative stories and poetry to discover and dwell in God's truth. Learning to see truth from the inside so that we are enabled to see the extraordinary nature of real life rather is the gift of stories. When we see the world charged with meaning in this way, we cannot help but respond in worship, joy and wonder. Seeing the world this way renews hope, too, hope that is not wishful thinking, but grounded in reality.

There is much more, however, than lists of favourite books in this exploration of writing. One chapter addresses God questions explicitly, as Sarah began theological study at Oxford. The experience was akin to floodgates being opened inside. 'Understanding rushed in to free me from fear and guilt and to widen my view of God's goodness.'[2] She lists theological books that have widened her view of God over the years, some of them classics, others yet to be tried and tested. They include titles that will be familiar to many Christian readers, such as Richard Foster's *Prayer: Finding the heart's true home*, while others are more demanding, such as N. T. Wright's *Jesus and the Victory of God*. True to her conviction that old books have as much to teach us as new ones, Irenaeus and Athanasius are there too. There are also books described that aim to help us navigate contemporary culture.

It is rightly claimed that a spirituality that does not drive us outwards to engage with the world is not a genuine Christian spirituality. What is a Christian response to a news bulletin that spends the majority of its time reporting the economic fortunes of this or that company and mentions briefly at the end that the insect population of the world is in such serious decline that it faces mass extinction in the next one hundred years? How we think about the world and act within it needs to be informed, and reading will help us to form attitudes that do more than make a brief noise and then die away forgotten and useless. There is a better way than criticizing from a spiritual ghetto or simply sticking our heads in the sand.

Growing a sense of wonder

We are created to learn, and we all have the capacity for wonder. We are enabled to flourish as we are immersed in truth. All this comes from God. The reader is helped to see that the wonder and yearning that we experience when we hear a piece of music or see a beautiful star or read a well-written novel are not distractions cunningly leading us away from God, but glimpses of his character designed to draw us closer to him. C. S. Lewis wrote about his own flashes of emotion in *Surprised by Joy*, and in *Book Girl* Sarah returns to the theme that has been so crucial in enabling her to grow and broaden her experience of God and the world.

It is said that when we get to heaven, the first question God will ask is, 'Did you enjoy my world?' In an increasingly busy and frenetic postmodern culture, how may we recapture that sense of wonder and stop ourselves from filling every moment with activity and missing the point of it all? One way is through reading; reading not to tick off another book on a list, but reading to savour, reading to stimulate thinking, the imagination and the emotions. Slow reading that turns from the page into meditation and into prayer as in *lectio divina*. Reading poetry that sees the inconsequential as the means of grace, stories that awaken our longings for what matters, writers who can shock us into paying attention and halt our frantic minds.

Sarah sees the capacity for learning as a gift that is 'holy, set in us all by a God who made us to respond, grow and discover through the power of language'.[3] She continues a little later, 'Words make worlds and the more words we encounter, the richer the concept of the world becomes, the more we are able to see what is possible.'[4] Words also give us the power to change the world, and she quotes C. S. Lewis and Madeleine L'Engle, two of her favourite authors, to show how reading gives us the power to name reality, shape it and do something to change it.

For Christians, the power of words is embedded throughout the biblical narrative. God the Word spoke and creation came into being. Before the world was made, the Word existed, and without the Word nothing could exist. God spoke again and again to individuals directly and through his prophets until the time came for the Word to become flesh. Paul urged his readers at Colossae to 'let the word of Christ dwell . . . richly' in them and to encourage one another with words in 'psalms, hymns, and spiritual songs' (Colossians 3.16).

Formed by stories

What it means to be human is a vital question for Christians to investigate. We could pick up a book on ethics to explore this. We could use our powers of observation. We certainly need to wrestle with the narrative of the Bible, but secular stories? Sarah is adamant that stories form us, and good stories help to form us in the image of

God. She has a love of what is known as fantasy literature and was brought up on C. S. Lewis's Narnia stories and J. R. R. Tolkien's *The Lord of the Rings*, among others. In a chapter entitled 'Books can stir you to action', she describes how her encounter with Tolkien's trilogy in her teens was a turning point in her idea of herself and her faith because that story helped her to perceive the epic narrative of Scripture, the real divine drama by which her own life was defined. Reading Tolkien, which was such a great and beautiful drama to her mind, helped her to see that the drama of Scripture was even greater and demanded a response from her:

> Tolkien's story helped me to recognize Scripture as my own story, the one in whose decisive battles I was caught, the narrative that drew me into the conflict, requiring me to decide what part I would play: heroine, coward, lover or villain.

Sarah went on to say:

> The choice was clear. I simply said yes – to believing in God's goodness despite pain, to acting creatively and lovingly even in discouragement, to fighting for light in the midst of whatever darkness I found myself.[5]

Are we all called to be heroines? Surely this sounds like romantic idealism? But:

> Heroism isn't about taking your own life in your hands; it's about being taken hold of by something much bigger and more beautiful than yourself, by a story that draws you into its larger drama and empowers you to act in hope.[6]

Many aspects of reading are explored in the book. It is a very personal view, and deliberately so. Sarah provides her 12 all-time favourites, which she admits was no easy task, but reading her comments on each choice is illuminating. She based her selection on books that have gripped and formed her as a person, broadened her world and inspired a sense of the possibilities of life. They include a favourite author of hers, Wendell Berry, who has something of a following in the USA though is less well known in the UK. A writer of novels and poetry, Berry lives on a farm in Kentucky, holds the earth in deep reverence and speaks out on environmental issues. There is much about the holiness of life and the small miracles of every day in his writing, and he sits comfortably with the writers represented here.

Books expand our horizons

Sarah's other books develop themes that have contributed to the formation of her life as a writer. They include *The Life-giving Home* and *Girls' Club*.

It is sometimes said that books make a home, and home is clearly important to Sarah. *The Life-giving Home* is a collaborative book, written by Sarah and her mother, with contributions from her brother Joel. There is a lot about teatimes, books and stories, traditions, spiritual rhythms and practices, feasting, celebrating life and understanding the importance of beauty to satisfy the soul. Colour, creativity and order are reflected in creation and the authors argue that our homes should reflect these qualities too. It is a book about hospitality from a home that welcomed many visitors over the years. Home was a place of welcome and the celebration of joy, but also a place of refuge, comfort and safety, a port in the storms of life.

Home was also the place where Sarah, her mother and her sister invented Girls' Club, an intentional commitment on the part of each of them to gather together regularly and grow in friendship and become kindred spirits to one another. The book of the same name that tells the story of it is really a book about deep friendship and how to foster it. It addresses the loneliness of our age that is so pervasive. Through telling their stories, one voice at a time, the three share the experience of growing up, sharing struggles and learning to be the women God made them to be.

It is clear that reading has enriched this writer and helped her find her own voice to express her take on life abundant.

Key themes
- Reading for reading's sake
- How reading forms us
- Truth, beauty and goodness
- Family and friends

Questions and action points
- Can you recall books from childhood that you loved and that shaped your view of the world?
- Are there key moments in your life that have been shaped by something you read? What impact has reading had on your faith?
- Sarah Clarkson's sense of self has clearly been nurtured by reading. Is there a character in a novel or a story that has helped you find a sense of identity or to choose the direction your life has taken so far?
- What would you include in your top 10 books? Top 20?
- In the introduction, the writer identifies the following three gifts of reading: filling our hearts with beauty, giving us strength for the (spiritual) battle and reminding us that we are not alone. What are the gifts of reading that you would want to pass on?
- When did you last recommend a 'good read' to someone else? What was it and why did you value its contents?
- Are there people in your life in whom you are seeking to foster the love of reading? How are you doing this?
- Does your church encourage reading as a spiritual practice?

- Is there a book that you love that is not among Sarah Clarkson's lists? Why would you want to include it?
- Consider starting a notebook of memorable quotations or key ideas from things you have read. Alternatively, you could incorporate this practice into a spiritual journal.

Writings

Book Girl: A journey through the treasures and transforming power of a reading life (Illinois: Tyndale Momentum, 2018).

Caught Up in a Story (Illinois: Tyndale Momentum, 2014).

Girls' Club, with Sally Clarkson and Joy Clarkson (Illinois: Tyndale Momentum, 2019).

The Life-giving Home, with Sally Clarkson (Illinois: Tyndale Momentum, 2016).

Read for the Heart (Illinois: Tyndale Momentum, 2009).

Website

<www.sarahclarkson.com/thoroughly-alive>

5

Annie Dillard:
the world is charged with
the grandeur of God

I first read Annie Dillard when a dear friend put a copy of *Pilgrim at Tinker Creek* into my hands.[1] From the opening lines I was captivated. Here was writing that sent tingles down my spine. Her acute powers of observation, coupled with her insight into the greater significance of ordinary things, did what all good writing should do: it enlarged my world. Of the writers represented in this book, Annie Dillard is one of the more prolific and also one of the most written about. She is the writer most often quoted by the other writers in this volume. She has been described as a mystic, a poet, an essayist, a novelist, a naturalist, a critic, a theologian, a collagist and a humorist. She has been analysed by academics in different disciplines, from literature to ecology. Some articles about her focus solely on her writing style and she is certainly a writer's writer. She has, after all, written a book about the trials and tribulations of writing, *The Writing Life*, and a book of literary theory, *Living by Fiction*.

Writing that is original

Annie Dillard is not easy to categorize. She calls herself an 'anchorite' in *Pilgrim* and a 'nun' in *Holy the Firm*, but these describe aspects of her life, not the whole, and neither is accurate on its own and out of context. Other readers and critics see things which may or may not be there. Annie herself warns on her personal web page to avoid all articles with the word 'eco' in them. They have nothing to do with her, she expostulates. She is connected to the Transcendentalists (see p. 73) and also to the Romantics in their immediacy and personalized epiphanies.

Anyone interested in these and other echoes of particular genres of writing will have plenty to explore. Here there is only space to note that her writing style uses strong verbs and bold rhythms, and she is liable to slide suddenly into parabolic mode. Often her sentences are as much poetry as prose. She is masterful at surprising the reader with a sudden comparison that makes us look at the ordinary in extraordinary ways. Here she is on writing in her own words:

> The line of words is a hammer. You hammer against the walls of your house. You tap the walls, lightly, everywhere. After giving many years' attention to these things, you know what to listen for. Some of the walls; they have to stay, or everything will fall down. Other walls can go with impunity; you can hear the difference. Unfortunately, it is often the bearing wall that has to go. It cannot be helped. There is only one solution, which appalls you, but there it is. Knock it out. Duck.[2]

A life in writing

Annie Dillard writes wonderfully about writing in *The Writing Life*, recounting its trials and the necessity of discarding so much that has been lovingly and painstakingly set down in order to achieve the final piece. She is clearly talking about herself, for she is constantly revising her work, writing and then rewriting, never finishing a piece for good. She paints a bleak picture of the writer's life, not at all the romantic image many of us conjure up. Describing the page as an eternal blankness and the activity of writing as 'ruining everything' even though there is nothing else for it, the sense of personal cost and the agonies of creativity are vividly portrayed.[3] All the same, it is the blank page that teaches one to write.

Annie Dillard is a writer who commands attention, whether or not we share her religious framework or are comfortable with the ease with which she reflects on what God is or is not up to in the world. In a 2007 review of her novel *The Maytrees* for the *Washington Post*, Marilynne Robinson observed:

> Annie Dillard's books are like comets, like celestial events that remind us that the reality we inhabit is itself a celestial event, the business of eons and galaxies, however persistently we mistake its local manifestations for mere dust, mere sea, mere self, mere thought. The beauty and obsession of her work are always the integration of being, at the grandest scales of our knowledge of it, with the intimate and momentary sense of life lived.[4]

Witnesses of wonder

As Annie herself pointed out in *Pilgrim*, 'Beauty and grace are performed whether or not we will or sense them. The least we can do is try to be there.'[5] She believes that we are put on the earth to be witnesses. This is a key theme of writers on prayer. Paying attention, being present, looking: all are essential to prayer that is about real life, and is authentic and real. Bearing witness seems such a vital part of what it means to be human, and the practice of it has fallen into abeyance, to our deep and lasting cost. Surely we would not have become so disconnected from the natural world and from each other if we had borne witness to the wonder of the earth and of human existence on it?

This reminds me of all the best poets and writers who not only write of beauty and wonder, but also describe the full range of human experience and response. Annie talks about 'seeing' and also of 'stalking', reminding us that a deepening awareness of the otherness of the natural world leads to a deepening awareness of our own dimensions, if only implicitly.

Mystery

This brings us to consideration of the term 'mystic', which is often applied to Annie Dillard. What is a mystic? The term is more misunderstood than appreciated, especially in Christian circles where it is thought to be all about private numinous experiences, the emphasis being on the experience itself.

The word *musterion* in the New Testament means 'that which was previously hidden' and is used in relation to the revelation of Jesus Christ (see Colossians 1.26–27). All the great mystics sought God, not experience for its own sake, and one of the ways God may be found is through the created world. Moses met God in a burning bush, Elijah on a mountainside in the 'sound of sheer silence' (Exodus 3; 1 Kings 19.11–12). Julian of Norwich spoke of the love of God as she saw it in her vision of a tiny hazelnut. Annie Dillard, in her turn, speaks of the wonder and majesty of God in the things that capture her attention. The Church still needs its mystics to remind us of the mysterious and unpredictable ways of the living God who is ever present for those with eyes to see.

Annie Dillard's first publication was a collection of poetry, *Tickets for a Prayer Wheel*, in 1974. We have already seen that there are connections between prayer and poetry, and one of my favourites among Annie's books is *Mornings Like This*, which she describes as 'found poems'. These are poems culled from catalogues, advertisements, jingles and the like which she has combed through 'like sculptors on trash heaps'.[6] One, entitled 'Learning to fear watercolor', gleaned from the instructions to Nicholson's Peerless watercolours, 1991, begins each short verse with a different colour. Each one, whether it be 'flesh tint' or 'sepia brown', comes with instructions on how to apply it. There is a warning with flesh tint, for example, on not getting the wash too strong, which begins, 'Be very careful.'[7] The whole is both amusing and startling at the same time and reads as if it is a carefully composed poem.

Seeing poetry as prayer and prayer as possessing poetic qualities may seem strange to anyone brought up with extempore prayer where one speaks from the heart. Such prayers are not carefully crafted liturgy in the tradition of Thomas Cranmer's collects, and the person praying is assured that God does not mind broken sentences and incorrect grammar. And he does not. But there are moments when a poem can speak for us in just a few compressed lines and express the deep longings of the human heart. Annie Dillard believes that poets and writers can be called to their work to illuminate the world. If the world is 'charged with the grandeur of God', as the poet Gerard Manley Hopkins insisted, we may expect to meet God there and be awed as we do so.

A God who defies our categories

Within the Christian tradition there are two great styles of praying that sound diametrically opposed but are open to anyone wanting to go deeper in prayer. Their technical names are cataphatic and apophatic prayer. Cataphatic prayer seeks God through concrete images: symbols, rituals, incense and visual imagery such as icons. Creation points to the Creator and the five senses are doors to perception of divine presence and activity. Apophatic prayer, conversely, seeks to be free of all images which are seen as distractions. The mind seeks stillness and freedom from sensual imagery until it reaches a simple state of being.

If cataphatic prayer is praying with one's eyes wide open, apophatic prayer is praying with the eyes shut. Annie emphasizes praying with our eyes open, bearing witness to God in his grandeur, majesty and wonder through the lens of creation. She refuses to sentimentalize creation, however, and in so doing our vision of God is denied domestication. We are not allowed to shrink God to our comfort zones. She says she gets angry with God when she sees so many people who seem to lack the organ by which they may perceive God. So, like Wordsworth and Coleridge, she will become a prophet of nature who will speak.

Annie Dillard is not the only author in this volume to be compared to her fellow American writers Walt Whitman and Henry David Thoreau, especially with respect to the latter's *Walden*, an account of his experience of living outdoors for a period. They were among the Transcendentalists, an idealistic philosophical and social movement which developed in New England around 1836 in reaction to rationalism. Influenced by Romanticism, Platonism and Kantian philosophy, Transcendentalism taught that divinity pervades all nature and humanity.

Annie Dillard is also sometimes co-opted to movements anxious about the future of the planet. While she might reject anything that contains the word 'eco' to describe her writing, her determination to make us look more closely at the natural world and learn makes her a crucial voice for our time as we grow more and more distant from the natural world we are in danger of destroying, not least through ignorance of it.

The real world

Anyone opening *Pilgrim* for the first time might wonder at the epithet 'humorist', for many of the descriptions of the cruelties of nature depicted in its pages are anything but funny. Within a few paragraphs Annie has described her cat jumping through the open window onto her chest in the middle of the night and leaving paw prints in blood all over her, which made her look as though she had been 'painted with roses'. A few pages later she writes:

> I had read about the giant water bug, but never seen one. 'Giant water bug' is really the name of the creature, which is an enormous heavy-bodied brown bug. It eats insects, tadpoles, fish and frogs. Its grasping forelegs are mighty and hooked inward. It seizes a victim with these legs, hugs it tight, and paralyses it with enzymes injected during a vicious bite. That one bite is the only bite it ever takes. Through the puncture shoot the poisons that dissolve the victim's muscles and bones and organs – all but the skin – and through it the giant water bug sucks out the victim's body, reduced to a juice.[8]

This is nature writing with no holds barred. Annie can nonetheless be very funny indeed. She enjoys jokes which she incorporates into her short essays on quirky subjects. In one she writes, 'On many fine mornings I do not concern myself overmuch with the mystery. And by controlling the depth of my thinking carefully, I permit myself a little joke.'[9] Perhaps this is a sign that she does not take herself too seriously, Pulitzer Prize notwithstanding.

Annie Dillard grew up in a family that loved jokes and words, their sounds and quirky usage. She was born in Pittsburgh, Pennsylvania, USA, in 1945. Most of the following biographical sketch comes from her memoir, *An American Childhood*, written in 1987, for as she says, 'The way to learn about a writer is to read the text. Or texts.'[10] There is something refreshingly liberating about this diktat, and while I found some of the articles about aspects of her writing fascinating, the discipline of reading Annie herself, fresh and undiluted, is a far better way to get to know her. That this is true for any writer goes without saying, yet most of us are so afraid of 'great' authors that we give in before we get started and read other people's thoughts instead. That, of course, is what I am doing here, but in the hope that these brief introductions will be sufficient to introduce a new name and create a thirst to read the original.

What is a great author? Some in this volume are widely known while others are just beginning their writing careers. Annie Dillard is one of the well-known writers whose readership spreads far beyond the confines of the Christian Church. Yet she in her turn introduces us to the writer and mystic Julian of Norwich and would surely be delighted that some of her readers go in search of Julian herself. There is a difference between endless critical studies of an author and a brief taster designed to entice. The invitation is to discover a new author and dive in, however startling the shock of the new.

Implicit faith

It is interesting to me that while some commentators view Annie Dillard as areligious, and in much of her writing religious faith is implicit rather than explicit, others, such as Marilynne Robinson and Eugene Peterson, view her as profoundly Christian and a voice that needs to be listened to by Christians everywhere. It is true that much of her writing needs time and repeated visits to get to the heart of what she is saying.

On her personal web page under 'Religion', Annie has 'None.'[11] Yet *Pilgrim* is named as being among the century's hundred best spiritual books. *Holy the Firm* is also clearly founded on theological themes. Writers have pointed out that in her memoir, *An American Childhood*, she wrote of how she came to treat visits to her local Presbyterian church with disdain. She wrote elsewhere that she overcame a fiercely anti-Catholic upbringing to escape Protestant guitars, but however disrespectful of religion she may sound, she goes to church anyway. 'I know only enough of God to want to worship him, by any means ready to hand . . . there is one church here, so I go to it.'[12] In her essay 'An expedition to the Pole', she compares going to church with being like going to the North Pole, and proceeds to relate some of the tragicomic stories of failed expeditions over the years. The amateurishness and blithe ignorance of so much that goes on in church frustrates her, but she goes anyway. She recognizes that, like an expedition to the Pole, faith cannot be practised in isolation.

The same friend who put *Pilgrim* into my hands also gave me *Holy the Firm*, with the words, 'I've no idea what it's about,' then added, 'but it's wonderful.' This, the most theological of her books, is a kind of poetic narrative inviting us to adopt a sacramental vision of the world, but it does not do so by the easy route of beauty. It tells the story of a little girl cruelly disfigured by an aeroplane crash. Over the course of three days spent on an island in Puget Sound, Annie reflects on creation, suffering and redemption through the eyes of the artist, the thinker and the nun. Peterson states that it 'wrestles pain to the mat in a wild, unforgettable agony'.[13]

Holy the Firm is a wonderful example of how to 'tell the truth but tell it slant', as the poet Emily Dickinson described it. It dispels any doubt that nature and the Christian tradition provide the framework for the way Annie Dillard sees the world. On the first day the writer awakens to the wonder of divine presence: 'Every day is a god, each day is a god, and holiness holds forth in time.'[14] The world for Annie is an illuminated manuscript that dazzles and draws her. Within the beauty of the new day are memories of pain and death as she recalls a moth flying into the flame and burning up. The next day a plane crashes and the pilot pulls his seven-year-old daughter from the wreckage alive, but as he does so some burning fuel hits her in the face and disfigures her terribly. Annie reflects that she had come to Puget Sound to study hard things and learn from them, but she had not bargained for this. How can she pray in such circumstances?

I sit at the window, chewing the bones in my wrist. Pray for
them: for Julie, for Jesse her father, for Ann her mother, pray.
Who will teach us to pray? The god of today is a glacier. We live
in his shifting crevasses, unheard.[15]

The faith-shaking questions tumble out of her and she refuses to
duck them. The third day finds her going to the local store to buy
communion wine in preparation for the service at the Congrega-
tional church nearby. She reflects on the medieval belief that there
is a created substance at the base of everything that is always deep
down and hidden where it is in touch with the Absolute. The substance is called 'Holy the firm'. Touching it holds us in God 'who has
a stake guaranteed in all the world'.[16] She names the wounded child,
with whom she feels an affinity, not least because they look a bit like
each other, Julie Norwich, alluding to the fourteenth-century an-
choress Julian of Norwich who had a series of visions as she lay in
acute pain and sickness. Julian spent the rest of her life meditating on
these visions and, in the face of terrible suffering, her own and that of
bleak and fearful times, she held on to the conviction that 'All shall
be well, and all shall be well and all manner of things shall be well.'

  In powerful prose, Annie Dillard addresses Julie Norwich out of
her own prayers, inviting her to live. At the same time she finds a re-
affirmation of her own vocation to prayer and sacrificial living. It is
this revelling in the glory of the created world, even as she wrestles
with the cruelty and apparent randomness of suffering, that makes
her a challenging, and for me a deeply grounded, writer, who helps
me to find my own courage to face the contradictions of living with
'eternity in my heart and the world beneath my feet'.[17]

Exegete of creation

Eugene Peterson devotes a whole chapter to Annie Dillard in his
book *The Contemplative Pastor* and addresses his thoughts to

'professional' Christians who are caught up in busyness. Using the words 'unbusy', 'subversive' and 'apocalyptic', he offers wisdom to live by in terms that might have been unearthed especially with Annie Dillard in mind.

Peterson claims that Annie is an exegete of creation in the same way that John Calvin was an exegete of Scripture: 'The passion and intelligence Calvin brought to Moses, Isaiah and Paul, she brings to muskrats and mockingbirds.'[18] He argues that the fact that she does not shrink from the dark side of nature but confronts it head on and writes about it boldly pushes her into the category of religious writing. She neither 'appreciates' nature nor sentimentalizes it. She does not try to 'explain' it either. 'These things are not issues; they are mysteries.'[19]

Peterson draws out a comparison between Annie Dillard and the medieval anchorites, men and women who withdrew from the world to pray and contemplate the ways of God in solitude. They lived in cells attached to churches. Annie herself describes her vocation as a blend of nun, thinker and artist, as *Holy the Firm* illustrates, a combination that is potential dynamite. The difficulty is that our western culture does not value nuns, thinkers or artists very much, yet it desperately needs them. 'A nun lives in the fires of the spirit, a thinker lives in the bright wick of the mind, an artist lives jammed in the pool of materials.'[20] She describes her cabin at Tinker Creek as an 'anchorhold'. It's a place to think (and there is a lot to think about as she observes nature before her eyes) and it holds her there and steadies her.

Peterson's main point in drawing attention to Annie's writing is to show how she has assimilated Scripture:

so thoroughly . . . that it is simply at hand, unbidden, as context and metaphor for whatever she happens to be writing about. She does not, though, use Scripture to prove or document; it is not a truth she 'uses' but one she lives.[21]

Nature and God's word

Scripture for Annie Dillard is nourishment for the praying imagination rather than fuel for apologetic argument. Nature and God's word thus come together, with the latter the wide world within which she gives her attention to the non-verbal world of creation. The biblical allusions are so many that it is easy to miss them.

The key word for understanding what she is trying to teach us is 'witness'. Witnesses may draw our attention to something simply by their own stance of paying attention themselves, but there is also an important place for articulating what we see. Annie Dillard suggests that putting things into language helps people to see better, a consequence that begins with the seer him or herself. I heard a lovely example of this recently as a mother spoke of a walk in the park with friends and their children. As they walked, one or another would draw attention to a tree, a flower or a passing butterfly. Suddenly, one of the adults who did not have young children exclaimed that she never normally noticed any of these things. No one drew her attention to them, and they escaped her notice. It also reminds me of the sad truth that as fewer and fewer people know the names of flora and fauna, they will never notice when species disappear for ever, let alone care about them.

In *Teaching a Stone to Talk*, Annie wrote about the palo santo trees on the Galapagos Islands: thin, pale and wispy lines of them standing in silence. It is not a silence of absence, however, but one of presence. They are a metaphor for witness, and she writes:

> The palo santos interest me as emblems of the muteness of the human stance in relation to all that is not human. I see us as palo santo trees, holy sticks, together watching all that we watch, and growing in silence.[22]

Annie Dillard might decry the prefix 'eco', but the following words not only demonstrate Peterson's point about the way her writing is saturated with Scripture, but also utter a wake-up cry that is so urgent and necessary for humanity to heed:

> We doused the burning bush and cannot rekindle it; we are lighting matches in vain under every green tree. Did the wind used to cry and the hills shout forth praise? Now speech has perished from among the lifeless things of earth and living things say very little to very few.[23]

Annie Dillard's memoir, *An American Childhood*, describes a happy state full of freedom to roam and explore on foot and by bicycle. Summers at Lake Erie are described:

> I rode past cantaloupe stands and truck farms planted in tomatoes. I rode past sandy woods and frame houses with green shutters and screened porches full of kids. I played baseball with some of the kids. I got a book on birds, took up bird-watching, and saw a Baltimore oriole in an apple orchard. I straddled my bike in amazement, bare feet on the cool morning road, and watched the brilliant thing bounce singing from treetop to treetop in the sun.[24]

Annie explains that when she was eight her family moved house, and she began a life of reading books, drawing and playing at the sciences. 'Here also I began to wake in earnest, and shed superstition, and plan my days.'[25] Here is the key understood by so many writers on the spiritual life, that to live each day well leads in turn to a life lived well. Learning to pay attention to the daily routines and the experience of living from day to day helps us to live deeply rather than on the surface of things and always looking for the next stimulant. The particular, or the small world, will lead her, Annie Dillard believes, to the meaning of her life. She moves easily from the grandeur of creation to the mundane, admonishing us to 'admire the world for never ending on you'.[26] Her gift is to help us see this for ourselves through her writing. As she puts it, 'Why are we reading if not in hope that the writer will magnify and dramatize our days, will illuminate us with wisdom, courage, and the possibility of meaning-fulness and will press upon our minds the deepest mysteries.'[27]

Here is a slightly different take on the closeness of the spiritual world and the down-to-earth dailiness of ordinary life from that of Kathleen Norris. Like Kathleen, Annie is reminding us of heaven's ever-present proximity if only we had eyes to see. This urgent plea is repeated throughout this volume, and, since most of us spend a lot of time with the small and insignificant things that make up a day, it is reassuring that meaning may be found there. The challenge is to look.

Key themes

- The grandeur and randomness of the natural world
- Beauty and cruelty in creation
- The craft of writing
- The mystery of life
- Praying with your eyes open
- The world of the Bible as the framework for seeing
- The sacramental nature of the world

Questions and action points

- In a chapter of *Pilgrim at Tinker Creek* entitled 'The present', Annie Dillard describes looking at a cedar tree and catching a momentary glimpse of glory which, as soon as she became conscious of it and articulated it to herself, vanished. Trying to recapture it after the moment had passed was as if it was a 'still-beautiful face belonging to a person who was once your lover in another country years ago: [it is recalled] with fond nostalgia, and recognition, but no real feeling save a secret astonishment that you are now strangers'.[28] How well do you think this captures the experience of trying to hold on to momentary experiences of joy?

- In the same section of *Pilgrim*, Annie concludes that experiencing the present moment purely 'is being emptied and hollow; you catch grace as a man fills his cup under a waterfall'.[29] How have you experienced grace-filled moments in your life so far?

- Annie Dillard advocates praying with our eyes wide open and being witnesses to the presence of God, for 'beauty and grace are performed whether or not we will or sense them. The least we can do is try to be there.'[30] Can you think of examples of beauty and grace in the world that seem oblivious to acknowledgement by human beings? Try practising praying with your eyes open, perhaps when out walking, and later record what you notice.

- Do you consider yourself to be a writer of any kind (from novels to jottings in a notebook)? Have you struggled to say what you want to say and kept trying till it felt OK? What kept you trying?

- Have you read any of the Christian classics written by so-called mystics? How did they convey what they had experienced? Did they resonate with your experience of God in any way? If you have not read Julian of Norwich or Teresa of Avila, try reading them and see if they provide new insights about God and the way God relates to us.

- Peterson describes Annie Dillard as an exegete of creation in the same way that Calvin was an exegete of the Bible, so that we become 'alert to God everywhere, in everything, praising, praying with our eyes open'.[31] Is there a writer who has done this for you? How did he or she achieve this?

Select writings

An American Childhood (New York: Harper and Row, 1987).
Holy the Firm (New York: Harper and Row, 1977).
Living by Fiction (New York: Harper and Row, 1982).

The Maytrees (New York: HarperCollins, 2007).

Mornings Like This (New York: HarperCollins, 1995).

Pilgrim at Tinker Creek (New York: Harper's Magazine Press, 1974).

Teaching a Stone to Talk (New York: Harper and Row, 1982).

Tickets for a Prayer Wheel (Columbia: University of Missouri Press, 1974).

The Writing Life (New York: HarperCollins, 1989).

Further reading

Eugene Peterson, *The Contemplative Pastor: Returning to the art of spiritual direction* (Grand Rapids: Eerdmans, 1989).

Richard G. Geldard (ed.), *The Essential Transcendentalists* (East Rutherford: Penguin, 2005).

6

Margaret Guenther: spiritual midwifery

Spiritual direction has been one of the major building blocks of my own spiritual life, so it is a joy to introduce Margaret Guenther, whose writing on spirituality and spiritual direction is so central to the renewal of this gift to the Church. I cannot recall whether I first read her book, *Holy Listening*, and then listened to her deliver a series of talks over three days or whether it was the other way round, but Margaret was gifted in speaking as well as writing.

Born in 1929 (died 2016), Margaret was Emeritus Professor at General Theological Seminary in New York City where she taught Ascetical Theology. She was also the Director of the Centre for Christian Spirituality, a pioneering programme for the training of spiritual directors. She was a sought-after retreat leader and lecturer both in the United States and abroad, and would travel as far away as China and Australia to speak at conferences and lead retreats. Margaret was ordained and was Associate Rector of St Columba's Church in Washington, DC in later life.

Later in the book, in Chapter 10, we will see how Barbara Brown Taylor focuses on her own quest to be faithful to God's call to be a human being. In contrast, Margaret Guenther focuses more on the examples of individuals who have crossed her path in their search for wholeness and healing. There is a large cast of characters who illustrate Margaret's gentle and humane ministry of spiritual directing. She explains that all the stories she relates are true, though they may be cut and pasted with names changed.

What is spiritual direction?

There is a certain amount of mystique around spiritual direction. For anyone who imagines that it is reserved for a few spiritual athletes, or that it is just another consumer-driven fad, *Holy Listening* would be a good introduction to this ancient Christian ministry which aims to encourage people's desire to pray. At its heart, spiritual direction is about one Christian accompanying another on the journey of discovering prayer.

Margaret begins her book by insisting that it is written by an amateur for amateurs.[1] Reclaiming the word 'amateur' as someone who loves the art that she serves and loves the Holy Spirit who is the real director in every case of genuine spiritual direction, she bathes her subject in an atmosphere of humility, which is as it should be. The director is not a guru with special access to God but a fellow traveller, at a different point on the road, perhaps, but as ordinary and fallible as any human being. She immediately takes us back to the Desert Fathers, who knew a lot about humility and about wise spiritual discernment (see Chapter 8 on Benedicta Ward).

Metaphors for spiritual direction

Margaret writes self-consciously as a woman, a wife and a mother, so it is interesting that her three chosen metaphors of spiritual direction are deeply rooted both in Scripture and in activities that women practise, though not exclusively. Each chapter begins with verses from the Bible, and she unpacks her images carefully with language that echoes the biblical narrative while also being filled with the everyday.

Spiritual direction involves telling our stories and making sense of where God is at work in the pictures that emerge. Margaret comments:

Like all of us, the person seeking spiritual direction is on a journey. Since the expulsion from Eden we have been a people on the move, despite attempts at self-delusion that we have somehow arrived. We follow in the footsteps of our peripatetic Lord, always on the way, our faces turned resolutely or reluctantly towards Jerusalem.[2]

The first chapter concerns the director as giver of hospitality. As the host, the spiritual director must keep her own house in order, spiritually speaking; she makes preparations to receive her guest as any host does, she places herself at the service of her guest and shares her space with him or her, physically and spiritually.

Hospitality

There are nice personal touches that bring to life what spiritual direction is about. Margaret recalls living in Switzerland, where taking a bath in her flat was difficult, so friends who had her to stay would show kindness by allowing her to wallow in luxury in their bathrooms. In the same way, part of spiritual direction is dealing with the rubbish in our lives: the secret sins, the unconfessed burdens and the desire for healing. Along the way we learn a great deal about the art of spiritual direction, the role of the director in listening, bearing another's burdens, and what is and is not appropriate self-disclosure.

For anyone wondering whether God might be calling them to this ministry, *Holy Listening* is the fruit of an experienced practitioner. For anyone wondering whether spiritual direction might be of benefit, the process is clearly laid out in the book. For those of us who have never encountered spiritual direction but have homes or are teachers or even midwives, there is much to ponder in this book about the opportunities these roles afford to discover God at work. Are we teachers, for example? Good teachers encourage play, know their pupils' limits, always have hope, ask questions and enable the pupils to embrace their questions, are able to evaluate progress, are willing to be vulnerable and always continue to be learners.[3]

Teacher

We learn a lot about Margaret in the chapter on the spiritual director as teacher, for teaching is a huge part of her life and calling. A spiritual director is simultaneously a teacher and a learner of discernment – that quality of mature humanity that we are all called to practise if we are to navigate life's twists and turns. The key question of spiritual direction, 'Where is God in this?', is about discerning what God is up to in our lives and takes spirituality directly out of the realm of anything esoteric or seeing it as an accessory to something fundamental to being alive. She examines Jesus' ministry in the Gospels, where there are more than 40 references to him as teacher. She sees the story of the rich ruler in Mark 10 as the paradigm for spiritual direction, especially for spiritual direction as teaching. 'Good Teacher, what must I do to inherit eternal life?' (Mark 10.17) is THE question that all of us seeking God have to grapple with.

Midwife

For me, the most intriguing chapter of *Holy Listening* is the one on the spiritual director as midwife. Perhaps it has something to do with the fact that my mother was a midwife, but more likely it is because pregnancy and giving birth had a profound effect on my theology. It is also a neglected metaphor of the spiritual life, and there are rich seams to be mined.

Margaret draws on biblical imagery, of which there is more than we might think, as well as *The Complete Book of Midwifery*[4] to make some remarkable parallels between giving birth in the physical and the spiritual realms. For example, in physical birth there is what is known as the 'transition' period, which comes at the end of the first part of labour and is the time of greatest discomfort and often shock and loss of control. How similar that is to spiritual times of transition that may arise from experiences such as loss, but may also come out of the blow when we discover that the old ways don't work any more. Yet this stage of spiritual life can lead into a new awareness and clarity, fresh growth emerging out of the seeming chaos and shifting ground. A midwife/director will help notice the signs and give encouragement and support.

The final chapter of *Holy Listening* is about women specifically and the unique gifts they bring to spiritual direction. Margaret wrote in the early days of a growing acceptance of women's ministry when much of it was still on the margins and in the cracks as far as the Church was concerned. It is a chapter to read and ponder as to how far we have come since then or not, and to ask ourselves whether we agree that women have something distinctive still to bring to the table, now that our ministry has been ritualized and institutionalized. Margaret also considers the fact that the majority of those seeking spiritual direction are women, and wonders about this.

The second half of life

Toward Holy Ground is about the questions that rise up in the second half of life. Margaret sets out to explore first how we can minister, befriend and accompany one another in the second half of life and then how we can shape our lives and discern the unique insights, gifts and opportunities of that part of life. While this sounds like a book written by a woman for women, I think men should address these issues with great urgency too.

Adopting the legendary grandmother of Jesus and mother of Mary, St Anne, as her role model for each theme, Margaret picks out some relevant points for this phase of life that we must attend to in order to grow spiritually. These include kinship, wholeness, harvest and fruitfulness, and a good death.

Margaret was writing in the 1990s, and since then there have been a number of books on the spirituality of ageing, but it remains a difficult subject for many, immersed as we are in a culture that is determined to cultivate the young and beautiful and avoid all issues around dying and old age.

The book is rich in content. The chapter on kinship, for instance, not only covers family, communities and spiritual friends, but also has a section on intercession that contains some of the most helpful practical ideas I have encountered. How do we pray for people who have hurt us or who wish us harm? And how do we pray for those whom we have hurt? And what has this got to do with kinship and the second half of life? Deep intercessory prayer opens us up to the pain of the world and our own impotence. We cannot pray for the world and then turn our back on it, for we are connected with it in all its joys and sorrows.

The chapter entitled 'Craft' begins with a reflection on spinning and weaving but goes on to discuss crafting a rule of life, something Margaret wrote a whole book about in addition to what is here. *At Home in the World: A rule of life for the rest of us* explores what this is all about. I have read many 'how to' books on constructing a rule of life and crafted a few of my own, but the approach here is the most fresh and freeing I have found. Rather than concentrating on creating grids and delineating topics for inclusion, Margaret focuses on broader concepts such as how we use our time and our energy. What would simplicity look like in our lives? How could we practise generosity in a regular way so that we grow in learning to make the gift of ourselves? A rule concerns how we relate to the world, how we continue to grow, how we avoid distractions that prevent spiritual growth. Since this topic comes up in *Holy Listening* as well as *Toward Holy Ground* and has a whole book to itself, it would seem that this is a fundamental aspect of Margaret Gunther's spirituality.[5]

Being fruitful

Toward Holy Ground especially resonated for me in the chapter called 'Healing, wholeness and harvest', where Margaret writes about being fruitful in the second half of life in the light of the barren women of the Bible: Sarah, Rachel, Hannah and Elizabeth, women who all saw themselves as deficient because they could not bear children. In their culture they were failures, but what does barrenness look like today when many women choose not to have children and are not judged on the basis of whether they are mothers or not? There remains a call to be fruitful, so what might it look like for God to remember us in maturity; what kinds of new life are we being called to bring forth? It could be a vocational change or simply going deeper in our walk of faith. It will certainly mean living passionately, being unafraid to feel, being open to both joy and pain, living generously.

It is poignant to read the chapter called 'A good death', since Margaret herself is now deceased. It is a short chapter, but a necessary one in a book about the second half of life. She writes with great sensitivity about loss and diminishment in old age and what we need to do to prepare to die well. She acknowledges that it is not easy to look into the abyss, but pretending we are not mortal is a lost opportunity. Quoting one of her favourite writers, Meister Eckhart, she refers to his sermon on the boy Jesus in the temple and the need to leave the crowd if we want to experience the birth of God in our soul. The 'crowd' here means all the distractions that keep us from God at the last. Dying is a solitary business, and Margaret wonders if, as explorers in Christ, we have to return to the ground from which we came. Thus we come full circle.

'Grund' is one of Eckhart's most used words. It suggests many things, including depth, darkness and the solidity of bedrock. It is our place of origin (Genesis 1). It is holy ground. This is the place to which, when the extraneous has been let go, we return. Quite possibly, Margaret writes, we are not fully grown up until just before our arrival, when we finally return to our origin and the holy ground from which we came.[6]

Rare parchment

Margaret Guenther also makes suggestions about how we should treat those who are old and near to death, referring to them as 'rare parchment waiting to be read'. If we sit and listen, they may be our teachers and our textbooks. The final chapter of *Toward Holy Ground*, in fact, is about ministry with the aged, something Margaret is well qualified to write about.

As with spiritual direction, listening in this context is key. I imagine her sitting with the elderly and the dying and listening with the utmost attentiveness to their stories. The spirituality of the aged is a spirituality of storytelling, she says.[7] I wonder what we miss when we relegate older people to the 'has-been' pile of life, ignoring their life's experience and the wisdom that has accumulated over the years. The Bible has things to say about the elderly that are both positive and negative. Old age does not guarantee wisdom, but among those who have paid attention to God and searched for meaning in the midst of life, there are precious things to be passed on.

There are not many books on prayer and spirituality that suggest filling a cup of tea for an elderly person in bed only two-thirds full since that's easier to handle, but Margaret mentions this as something a visitor might do to be helpful and to maintain the person's dignity at one and the same time.

Walking as spiritual practice

In her little book *Walking Home: From Eden to Emmaus* Margaret wrote a series of reflections on walking, each one based on a passage of Scripture and each one earthed in human experience. This would make a good companion for Lent; indeed, my second-hand copy was divided by its former owner into 'weeks', suggesting a devotional theme for Lent.

In this book, Margaret is not afraid to argue with God and the way things turn out for some of the characters, such as Eve or Abraham and Isaac on the mountain of sacrifice. She wonders about what happens next in some of the stories, such as that of Hagar. She ponders on how looking back can sometimes be good in her chapter on Lot's wife – remembering what God has done for us, for example.

I love the humanity of this book and the permission to wonder imaginatively about what the Bible stories do not tell us. The chapter on the Flight into Egypt has Mary and Joseph leaving in haste with no time to buy supplies, the author wondering what, if anything, they took with them, seeing them struggle with an alien culture and language and wondering what they talked about on the way. All the way through, we are invited to ponder the meaning of the stories for ourselves and to apply them to our own walking of the way of faith, however often we stumble or take a wrong turn.

We learn a lot about the author's own life and walk of faith here, how she experienced her own Egypts and the need for an exodus, what it was like to move to a strange land with two small children where she did not know the language, bringing up her children, growing older. Sometimes she relocates the story to her home environment and tries to imagine, for example, Jesus walking along the road that runs past her house, accompanied by his friends on a hot summer's day.

We are encouraged, too, to empathize with others who are undergoing experiences similar to biblical ones, such as exile. We are invited to enter in to the experiences being described in biblical narratives such as that of Mary on her way to visit her cousin Elizabeth:

> This is a walk unlike any other in Scripture: she is not fleeing from slavery, nor leaving home like the Prodigal Son, nor has she been exiled from paradise. She is on her own, maybe for the first time in her life, compelled to act out of her own strength.[8]

A large proportion of the chapters are about journeys Jesus made. He was always walking, and Margaret invites us to eavesdrop on scenes such as the encounter with Bartimaeus or the walk to Emmaus. The latter gives rise to a reflection on the importance of telling our stories over and over in order to make sense of them and to find meaning in them. She concludes the book with the observation that 'Jesus just shows up with no appointment and not dressed as we expect. He refuses to look the part as he walks among us.'[9]

Key themes

- Spiritual direction
- Ageing well
- God in the midst of life
- Patterns for living/Rule of life
- Prayer and contemplation
- Women's spirituality

Questions and action points

- *Holy Listening* ends with a brief reflection on listening. Do you see yourself as a good listener? Can you recall times when you felt you were not listened to? What did that feel like? And how does it feel when you are listened to deeply?
- Do women experience God differently from the way men experience him? What is your experience of this? What are the defining factors of your spirituality?
- Do you regard yourself as more of a practical person or someone who enjoys spending time in prayer, worship and/or silence? Does Margaret Guenther's writing encourage you to see how both are necessary and important? How could you strengthen the side of you that feels weaker at present in ways that bring the two together?
- In *Walking Home*, the author reimagines Bible stories as if they were happening in her own context. Take a favourite story from one of the Gospels and reimagine it in your context. Imagine

what might be said by the characters involved and try to picture what is happening as the story unfolds.

- Spirituality in the second half of life includes reflections on dying as well as ageing. Is this something you have thought about in the way Margaret approaches it? How might the elderly teach us about holy ground?

Select writings

At Home in the World: A rule of life for the rest of us (New York: Seabury Books, 2006).

Holy Listening (London: Darton, Longman and Todd, 1992).

My Soul in Silence Waits: Meditations on Psalm 62 (Cambridge, MA: Cowley Publications, 2000).

The Practice of Prayer, The New Church's teaching series, vol 4 (Cambridge, MA: Cowley Publications, 1998).

Toward Holy Ground: Spiritual direction for the second half of life (Cambridge, MA: Cowley Publications, 1995).

Walking Home: From Eden to Emmaus (Harrisburg: Morehouse Publishing, 2011).

Website

7

Sister Margaret Magdalen: avoiding mediocrity

Sister Margaret Magdalen's books are very explicitly about prayer and the Christian life, with a deep focus on Jesus and his prayer. They are replete with biblical quotations and aim to teach without ever being 'preachy'. She writes to help readers deepen our experience of Jesus Christ, and therefore her books fit into the category of prayer and discipleship.

Imagination

Although her writing style is explicitly Christian and the kind of faith-based paperback that many people read, Sister Meg, as she is known, has some unusual features that make her books stand apart. In her first book, for example, the preface by Dr Michael Green, a prominent evangelical and evangelist, refers to her 'biblically controlled imagination' and 'loyalty to Scripture'.[1]

Imagination and biblical soundness are not always regarded as compatible, but for Christianity to be credible today, we must take the imagination seriously as a gift and an instrument for being fully human. Sister Meg's writing in this sense has a prophetic element about it. Ignatian spirituality has made a huge contribution to the way Christians pray with the Bible, and one of Ignatius' tools for engaging with God through his word was the imagination. He urged his retreatants to enter in to the stories, especially those in the Gospels, as if we are present and to each time end with a colloquy or conversation with the Lord Jesus. For a visual and sensual culture such as ours, this is a vital way of connecting Christian faith with life as it is lived.

Throughout her writings, Sister Meg draws on the Christian tradition in all its breadth, showing over and over how earlier teachings on prayer and the spiritual life continue to speak today. This has become more and more important in a rootless society and for a Church seeking new ways to address the longings and spiritual barrenness of today. For people coming to faith in adulthood, too, there is a need to put down roots deep into the Church's rich history of prayer and worship. Books like those written by Sister Meg help us to do that in fresh ways.

Sister Meg is a Baptist by background. She worked overseas in mission in what was then Zaire, now the Democratic Republic of the Congo. She also lectured in a college of education and then became an Anglican religious sister. I first encountered her writing when searching for good Lent material and I picked up her book *A Spiritual Check-up: Avoiding mediocrity in the Christian life*. Earlier in the twentieth century, Methodist minister Dr W. E. Sangster wrote a series of searching questions about our hidden lives and relationships with God, which he called *A Spiritual Check-up*.[2] I found that Sister Meg's book complemented his by encouraging us to see that God has been at work in our lives already, as well as what more there is to do.

Anatomy of spiritual growth

I have always been used to physiological terminology, since both my parents worked in the medical world and our home contained a number of graphically illustrated medical textbooks which I loved poring over as a child. Ears, nose and throat, not to mention bowels and livers, were familiar terms, and I knew more about human anatomy than many children of my age. The connection between the human body and the spiritual life is therefore intriguing, and we learn a lot about the amazing organism that is the human body. That is not the point of the book, but it roots spiritual growth firmly in human existence that is physical as well as spiritual.

Why have a spiritual check-up? We do not leave our cars to run and run until they go wrong, but have regular servicing to ensure that all is in good working order. A medical check-up is also a useful means of prevention, but most of us go to the doctor only when something is wrong. A spiritual check-up will inevitably bring to light things that need attention, but God in his kindness does not show us all our sinfulness at once, as it would be so overwhelming we could not cope. Instead, God's desire for us is that we grow, and so, bit by bit, we are shown what is needed for this to take place in a healthy and progressive way. We may need spiritual surgery. Our fears and our secret sins need to be dealt with, but God does this with holy love.

Recalling our baptism

First of all, Sister Meg sets out her method: recalling our baptism and going through it in slow motion. She uses the symbol of immersion, encouraging us to imagine going down into the waters of baptism and pressing pause at various points until we are plunged completely into his passion, death and resurrection and then rising up once more to walk in newness of life. Whether we were baptized as infants or as adults and can therefore remember it, we are all able to imagine being slowly immersed in deep water. The author says that this is a meditative process and we should expect to hear God speaking to us at each stage a word of challenge or rebuke, encouragement or praise.

This needs to be a process done over time, so *A Spiritual Check-up* is not designed to be a one-off, quick read. It is vitally important to listen to what God is saying as we focus on each part of the anatomy. Reading the book in a group, as Sister Meg suggests, is a good way of learning to grow together in Christ through building trust and confidence in listening to God. It could also put in place some accountability, especially in the light of all that she mentions as possible things God might say to us, for listening to him might lead into prayers of thanksgiving and penitence, culminating in a resolve to take certain actions. These might be in order, for example, to sharpen our zeal where it has become blunted, to put right some of the wrongs we have committed, to apologize, to seek to be reconciled, to go out to another person in loving service, to withdraw from someone whose greatest need is for a period of solitude, to protest against some injustice, to encourage the brave efforts of somebody, to take someone to task if that seems necessary, and to be far more sensitive to the needs and aspirations, the sufferings and longings of others.[3]

Redeemed feet

Sister Meg begins, naturally, with the feet, and we are invited to consider all the different places our feet have taken us with their spring and lift. Sister Meg then goes to the Scriptures to see what they have to say about feet. From Jesus' words, 'Follow me', with their immediacy and call to step out straightforwardly in the direction that the Lord leads, we are asked to consider whether we are still moving forward on our journey, or whether we have been invalided out.

Ezekiel 1.7 (KJV) speaks of 'straight feet', and Sister Meg notes that our spiritual feet can be as crooked and calloused as our physical ones. We can be flat-footed, plodding painfully along rather than with a spring and eagerly setting out in the way of God's commands. She turns to Isaiah 59 where the prophet speaks of the injustice and oppression all around and asks: Have our feet run to evil? Do we contribute to what Isaiah terms the 'desolation and destruction . . . in their highways' (verse 7), for example, on the roads by pressing our feet too hard on the accelerator?

Where we might distance ourselves from some of the grand gestures of going to the trouble spots of the world to act as a peacemaker, this brings our discipleship right down to earth in our daily actions.[4] Not that we are let off asking God whether he wants us to do something like that and have 'courageous feet'. 'How beautiful . . . are the feet of him who brings good tidings' (Isaiah 52.7, RSV) leads us to consider our willingness to witness to God's love and asks whether we are glad to bring good news, or are we more likely to take secret delight in running from one to another with the latest bad news? Ouch! This is not spirituality for wimps. Sister Meg does not leave us wincing, but rather invites us to dedicate each part of our body to the Lord afresh. So we thank God for all the good places our feet have brought us to as well as asking forgiveness for those places we should never have gone and we offer them in readiness to wherever God wants us to go, even to the valley of shadow.

Reference to our feet as 'hinds' feet' occurs three times in the Old Testament (Psalm 18.33; Habbakuk 3.19; 2 Samuel 22.34, all KJV) which seems significant. The author applies the image to those in particular who are required to exercise leadership in either secular or Christian circles as they need God's help to tread the heights safely and be protected from falling.

The chapter ends with reference to Jesus washing feet, the only part of the anatomy he washed, according to the Gospels, and we are bidden to picture him washing our feet and to pray the prayer included there.[5] As a sample chapter, this sets the pattern for the whole book.

Redeemed 'reins'

Chapter 4 moves to the ankles and so on up the body. Sister Meg not only includes the outward and visible parts of our bodies, but also those on the inside: sexual organs, womb, kidneys, liver, stomach, heart and mind.

Sexual organs might be an obvious subject for a spiritual check-up, but kidneys requires a bit more digging perhaps. Here we see how richly Sister Meg has been able to mine the Scriptures for wisdom concerning our growth into Christlikeness. The kidneys are often called 'reins' in the Bible and are thought of as the seat of motivation. Our adrenal glands are situated at the top of the kidneys and the adrenalin they secrete helps the body deal effectively with stress. Stress is a word used far more now than when this book was first published, so here is a very relevant study of something that is a physical killer, but what does this section have to teach us about the spiritual life? We are often conscious of adrenalin when we are faced with a sudden crisis or need for great courage. The adrenalin pumps round our bodies to prepare us for flight or fight. Our adrenal glands are merciful glands: without them we would never survive, for we could not flee danger or face difficult and stressful situations.

The kidneys, according to the writers of Scripture, govern our motives, and through the motivation our consequent actions. Six Bible verses follow, inviting God to search and examine the 'reins': the first five are Psalm 7.9; Jeremiah 11.20; 17.10; 20.12 and Revelation 2.23 (all KJV). Sister Meg then points us to Matthew 5.8, the Beatitude 'Blessed are the pure in heart: for they shall see God' (KJV). The Greek for 'pure', *katharos*, originally meant 'clean', but could also be used of purging. Its root meaning is unadulterated, unmixed, unalloyed. Thus the Beatitude could be translated as, 'Blessed is the person whose motives are absolutely pure, entirely unmixed and untinged with anything petty or selfish or devious, for that person will see God.'[6] This is a most demanding stance to aspire towards. Job spoke of how God 'cleaveth [his] reins asunder' and does not spare him (John 16.13, KJV).

Sister Meg reminds us of the words from Hebrews 4 where the word of God is described as 'living and active, sharper than any two-edged sword, piercing until it divides soul from spirit, joints from marrow; it is able to judge the thoughts and intentions of the heart' (Hebrews 4.12). Are we even aware, she asks, how mixed our motives are on so many occasions, even when we think we are operating out of our best ones?

Being known by God

At this point, Sister Meg asks an important question that concerns a key theme in Christian spirituality: How do we feel about knowing that God sees us exactly as we are? Does it fill us with dread and fear or are we comforted by the knowledge that nothing about us can make God withdraw his love from us? Do we feel hounded by the idea that there is nowhere we can go to hide from God's presence, as Psalm 139 makes so clear, or do we rest peacefully because of it?

Here we are invited to ask God to search us and try us; to aim his arrow of scrutiny on any particular target of our integrity.[7] The writer suggests doing so with a trusted friend and taking time over it, always calling to mind the words of Jeremiah: 'the steadfast love of the LORD never ceases, his mercies never come to an end; they are new every morning; great is thy faithfulness' (Lamentations 3.22–23, RSV).

This is definitely a book to take slowly, perhaps for Lent, but it will repay rich rewards in doing so. At the end, our whole being will have been dipped in God and created afresh. Sister Meg notes that certain words keep recurring in the book, words such as integrity, compassion, faithfulness, obedience, receptivity, service, watchfulness, joy and self-control. Which ones speak to us directly? We are called to a radical, Gospel-shaped life, and to respond to that call is to live all of life with a love-longing that expresses itself in total givenness.[8]

Jesus' prayer life

Anyone's private prayer life is holy ground, but what of the prayer life of Jesus? Can we know anything of this at all? In *Jesus, Man of Prayer*, Sister Meg writes of Jesus the mystic; Jesus the contemplative; Jesus the intercessor; Jesus the faithful son of Abraham, recipient of the Hebrew Scriptures and liturgy of his faith; Jesus who wept in prayer and cried out in bewilderment to his Father; Jesus who prayed redemptively through the unquenchable, unconquerable love that flowed from him towards those who hated him; Jesus who committed himself utterly to his Father and whose ceaseless aspiration was to glorify him.[9] Studying the prayer life of Jesus should quicken our own desire to pray and increase our sense of urgency about this aspect of our discipleship.

Each chapter of the book carries a title that is a brief phrase from the New Testament, more often than not words of Jesus himself. Jesus had an advantage over children who are born and raised one step removed from the natural world, as so many are today. Nature teaches us to be attentive. Think of a child searching for pebbles on the beach or watching an insect on a leaf. Jesus clearly had an intense interest in the natural world. In the first chapter on the senses and prayer, Sister Meg avoids the temptation to sentimentalize the natural world in the experience of Jesus. As well as speaking about the lilies of the field and the birds of the air, Jesus experienced the physical struggle of the desert and the hardness of the city, for Jerusalem made him weep with longing and sorrow. His anguish here was his prayer, Sister Meg points out.[10] She quotes the twentieth-century theologian Teilhard de Chardin:

> God, in all that is most living and incarnate in Him, is not far away from us, altogether apart from the world we see, touch, hear, smell and taste about us . . . He is at the tip of my pen, my brush, my needle – of my heart and of my thought.[11]

Sister Meg adds that, for Jesus, it was not the pen, the brush or the needle, but the saw, the plane and the hammer.[12] In the book as a whole we have an incarnational approach to prayer grounded firmly in the incarnation itself.

Abba, Father

Sister Meg writes beautifully about the way Jesus' teaching addresses God as *Abba*, Father, thus from the start emphasizing that prayer is about a relationship. She traces just how new this form of address was for Jesus' followers and how it carries with it so many aspects: dependency, intimacy, love and belonging to a family. She also shows how the relationship between Jesus and his *Abba* summed up his entire identity. Balancing the deeply personal prayer of intimacy was Jesus' practice of liturgical prayer, praying with his Jewish inheritance in the synagogue and at home. We are encouraged to see the value of liturgical prayer and the way it reminds us that prayer is not about feeling good so much as obedience.

In the chapter 'As it is written', we are shown the biblical character of Jesus' praying. No one knew better than Jesus God's communication of himself through his word. Pondering the way he would have learned the Scriptures, the author comments, 'whilst he was God's Word, he found his identity and vocation through God's word'.[13] Jesus repeatedly turned to the Scriptures for his authority in what he said and did. Sister Meg imagines the young Jesus encountering the Scriptures, pondering them and seeking to discern what they were saying. She wonders, for example, what the young Jesus made of the servant passages in the prophet Isaiah and then imagines him, as he grew older, dwelling more on these passages, meditating on them and immersing himself in them. She traces his development through the one incident recorded for us by Luke of his youth, then his baptism and temptation and his first public statement in the synagogue (Luke 4). If Jesus grew in understanding who he was through meditation on the Scriptures, that will be our experience too. We discover what it means to be a child of God, a member of Christ's body, what the Holy Spirit does in us and so on by dwelling in the Scriptures as Jesus did.

This chapter touches on both Ignatian prayer and *lectio divina* – two forms of prayer explored by other authors in this volume (see Sarah Clarkson on *lectio divina*, for example). It explores the importance of using the Psalms in our praying, as Jesus did, and imagines him seeing himself in them as he prayed in solidarity with his own people.

Sister Meg acknowledges that for most of us it is not realizing the importance of opening ourselves up to God's word that is the issue, but finding the time and the means of doing it. One possible incentive to persist in carving out time for God in prayer and Bible meditation might be her own description of us as people who are called 'like Mary to be a hollowed out space for the word; called to be obedient to it; called to say, "let it be to me according to your word", called to be a silence in which his Word may be heard'.[14] There is a structured meditation on the word in the appendix for this chapter, which leads us prayerfully through different aspects of its meaning.[15]

The humanity of Jesus

In *The Hidden Face of Jesus: Reflections on the emotional life of Christ*, Sister Meg uses her imagination to go behind what we know in the Gospels in order to explore what may be implicit there regarding the psychological make-up, emotions and imaginative world of Jesus. She regards this as speculative theology, but not in an academic or technical sense. Sister Meg is aware that this could be misconstrued as going beyond what is legitimate. She claims a desire to be loyal to biblical truth and that her writing is the fruit of prayer and reflection on the life of Jesus. She is adamant that what we know of Jesus by faith must of necessity be rooted in history (she was writing around the time of a debate over the supposed discrepancies between the Jesus of history and the Jesus of faith). The aim of the book is to make Jesus more real and more accessible to people who might otherwise fall prey to the common misconception of saying that Jesus is both divine and human but consciously or unconsciously approaching him as though he were really more divine. The result is a more distant Jesus whom we do not come to know personally. A Jesus who is distant will not challenge us to know ourselves and what it means to be fully human.

We know very little of the childhood and adolescence of Jesus – only that single incident, in fact, recorded by Luke. The writer reflects that by the time this took place, Jesus had made a very long inward journey as well as the outward one during that first Passover.[16] He returned to Nazareth with his parents and grew in stature and favour with God (Luke 2). He had to grow 'in knowledge, in character, in understanding, through relationships, the circumstances and vicissitudes of life, through pain – for inevitably he had his share of disappointments, sadness, misunderstandings and being misunderstood, through betrayals and the rough and tumble of school life'.[17]

Pondering this, for me, does two things. It reminds me of my own struggles growing up and the influences that led to the various choices and reactions I made as I moved through those years. That helps me to understand better the influences that I can thank God for and those for which I need to pray for forgiveness or let go of with grace. It also helps me to see Jesus as a fully human being 'who in every respect has been tested as we are', as Hebrews 4.15 puts it, and this makes him more real, more accessible and more able to stand with me in my own situations in life. He is not a God who is out there looking down in power, but a God who stands with me, who 'gets it' completely because he has been there and who does not show up my shortcomings so much as offer grace that makes me want to be more like him. Becoming like Jesus thus is something I do in my humanity rather than transcending it to become 'unreal' in this world's terms.

Mary Magdalene: a passionate woman redeemed

Another book by Sister Meg is about Mary Magdalene, a Gospel character who is often the subject of much confusion and misunderstanding. Sister Meg identifies Mary of Magdala, Mary of Bethany and the sinful woman of Luke 7.36–50 as the same person, something most New Testament scholars would eschew. Sister Meg argues that she is following liturgical tradition and is writing a book for devotional reflection rather than critical scholarship in order to lead us deeper into the mysteries of God's transforming work in human life. For some readers, this approach may detract from the message of the book, which is a pity because the subject Sister Meg addresses is that of transformed passion as an essential and God-given aspect of the spiritual life.

The relationship between earthiness and holiness challenges the dualistic thinking of many Christians where sexuality and spirituality are concerned. Sister Meg rescues the word 'passion' itself, so often imbued with negative connotations, and invites us to see it as cause for celebration. Most of us are fearful of the passionate side of human nature, but, as with the imagination, it is part of our creatureliness, and redeemed passion enables us to love courageously. Mary Magdalene, first apostle of the resurrection, was transformed by love, and her life has much to teach us about passion, penitence, brokenness and freedom. God calls us to a life of freedom and joy in a passionate, holistic and holy life.

The image of a dance forms the final chapter, where Sister Meg reflects on the implications of Jesus telling Mary not to 'cling' but to let go. It is a moving and powerful reflection on the power of love that sets us free.

I noticed again and again how Margaret Magdalen acknowledges the importance of others in the writing of her books, especially members of her community and those who helped with her writing. It is clear from the prefaces written by others that they in turn value Margaret for herself and rejoice in her wisdom and friendship. It seems that she herself embodies much of the spirituality she has been advocating in her writing, and so she and her books are all of a piece.

Key themes

- Jesus and his praying life
- Integrity in the spiritual realm
- The unswerving love of God
- The call to Christian maturity
- Avoiding mediocrity in the spiritual life
- Imagination and Scripture

Questions and action points

- Do you regard yourself as spiritually fit? How does the idea of a spiritual check-up appeal to you?
- How do you feel about God knowing you exactly as you are?
- Does Sister Meg's suggestion that, like Mary, we may become 'a hollowed out space for the word; called to be obedient to it' stir a desire to spend time with God? How could you make space for this?
- What have you learned about prayer through the prayer life of Jesus from Sister Meg's writing as described here? How could it help you to pray?
- How do you feel about using the imagination in the way Sister Meg does in her writing? Seek out a book about praying with the imagination, such as Gerard Hughes, *God of Surprises*,[18] or explore Ignatian approaches to prayer, such as James Martin, *The Jesuit Guide to (Almost) Everything*,[19] to help you get started.

- Are there people you know who live a passionate, holistic and holy life that exhibits joy and freedom? Do you have experience in your own life of redeemed passion that enables you to love courageously? Is this an area of life that you could bring to God in prayer, perhaps with the help of a Christian friend or spiritual director?

Writings

The Hidden Face of Jesus: Reflections on the emotional life of Christ (London: Darton, Longman and Todd, 1994).

Jesus, Man of Prayer (London: Hodder and Stoughton, 1987).

A Spiritual Check-up: Avoiding mediocrity in the Christian life (Godalming: Highland, 1990).

Transformed by Love (London: Darton, Longman and Todd, 1989).

8

Sister Benedicta Ward: with all the saints

Words can reach across time and bind us together with all the saints. Reading the prayers, thoughts and other writings of our Christian forebears helps to form our identity as the body of Christ.

I was an undergraduate studying history at Durham and took an optional paper on the early church in the theology faculty. There I was introduced to the Desert Fathers via the translations and commentaries of Sister Benedicta Ward. From that moment I realized that, for me, history and prayer would always be connected in a tangible way as I learned from the giants of the past what it means to 'put on Christ' (see Romans 13.14). The lives and writings of men and women from history, especially from the history of Christianity in the British Isles, began to offer up their treasures as I read and studied them. In so many ways their lives were different from mine: monks of the Egyptian desert, a monk-historian who hardly ever left his north-eastern monastery, a female solitary walled up in East Anglia, a Norman-French abbot who became Archbishop of Canterbury.

Could these distant individuals have anything to say to me, growing up in the twentieth century and wondering what prayer was really about? I had been led to believe that the Church had slept between its early beginnings and the time of the sixteenth-century Reformation, so I had a lot to learn. Here were individuals from the earliest times on who had wrestled with faith and the impact of the Christian gospel on their lives. They were very like us, despite living in such different times, and had the same concerns as Christians in every age.

History and holiness

With 14 books and numerous articles and book chapters, Sister Benedicta's main areas of interest converge on Christian holiness from late antiquity to the High Middle Ages. She covers individuals like St Anselm and the Venerable Bede, movements like the monks of the desert, and themes such as miracles in the medieval world. Her writings lead me to ask, when does a subject like history tip over into spirituality?

Could the same crossover happen with biology or English literature? I think the answer is yes in all cases, for 'all truth is God's truth',[1] and the spiritual practice of finding God in all things suggests that the divine is found everywhere. Theology may be described as thinking God's thoughts after God, but it is humans who divide the world into categories and subjects, and the theological angle is not confined to one small part.

Sister Benedicta tackles head on the difficulties over the word 'spirituality'. In a number of places she discusses the meaning of the word and how it has changed in usage. In the preface to *High King of Heaven: Aspects of early English spirituality*, she notes that none of the people she writes about in that book – Celts, Romans, Anglo-Saxons or indeed any medieval Christian – would recognize the word. She urges caution about the way modern usage often implies the non-material aspect of things, as in 'the spirituality of nature', and eschews the way it refers only to inner and personal experience as opposed to theology, doctrine and liturgy. By spirituality, she says, she means 'what the Anglo-Saxons [in this case] thought and said and did and prayed in the light of the Gospel of Jesus Christ'.[2]

She adds another important point, not often noted, that we can only ever access the outward reflections of a person's inner depth, especially, perhaps, at such a distance in time and context, although the same holds true even of those we think we know well. In reading about the spiritual lives of others and reflecting on their prayers, including those close to us and people of our own time, we cannot know the inner depths of another human being's relationship with God, for each one of us is unique and our deepest self is known only to God.

Friends in antiquity

Benedicta's historical characters came to life for me through her introductions and the way she presents them in their own words. Her latest publication, *Give Love and Receive the Kingdom*,[3] brings together essays on a number of figures from the history of spirituality, and in her introduction she calls them 'friends'.[4] A number of the writers here refer to other writers as if they are dear friends (for example, Sarah Clarkson). Her writings thus led me to read the writings of her subjects, who thereby became my friends too.

The Desert Fathers and Mothers are among the more exotic of subjects for the study of spirituality, at least to our contemporary minds. They were the first Christians who adopted a monastic lifestyle, living sometimes as hermits, sometimes in community, and they dwelt in the deserts of Egypt, Syria and first-century Palestine. Their lives seem strange to us now, but they appeared strange to their contemporaries too, arousing the same kind of criticism that is sometimes levelled at them today. Nevertheless, whenever there has been a crisis within the Christian Church, their wisdom and their desert context has yielded insight that gets to the heart of the matter. Perhaps this is because, above all, they went into the desert to learn how to be still and silent and to know themselves before God. They went seeking God, not experiences. Their sayings and the stories about them – the two main types of text that survive to tell their place in history – are hugely practical, concerned with actions, not mystical experiences.

From the Desert Fathers and Mothers we learn about the obedience required of a monk and the centrality of humility, forgiveness and charity. Examples of hospitality, of putting a fellow monk's welfare before one's own, and of self-control are what made the monks bear witness to the good news of the gospel. They were getting ready for the coming of God's kingdom, and in the desert they watched and endured in anticipation. They were in the main young and uneducated. They did not have copies of the Bible to hand or churches in which to worship, but they internalized the Scriptures through memory and spent long periods of time meditating on them, ruminating on the meaning and then putting into practice what they found there. Their sayings are often disarmingly simple, but they can also be extremely oblique and need to be pondered before they yield their wisdom.

We know about the desert dwellers through their sayings and through stories about them that were collected and brought to the western Church. Here are some examples:

A brother at Scetis committed a fault. A council was called to which Abba Moses was invited but he refused to go to it. Then the priest sent someone to say to him, 'Come for everyone is waiting for you.' So he got up and went. He took a leaking jug, filled it with water and carried it with him. The others came out to meet him and said to him, 'What is this, father?' The old man said to them, 'My sins run out behind me and I do not see them, and today I am coming to judge the errors of another.'[5]

Abba Pambo asked Abba Anthony, 'What ought I to do? And the old man said to him, 'Do not trust in your own righteousness, do not worry about the past, but control your tongue and your stomach.'[6]

If you see a man pure and humble, that is a great vision. For what is greater than such a vision, to see the invisible God in a visible man?[7]

A brother came to Scetis to visit Abba Moses and asked him for a word. The old man said to him, 'Go, sit in your cell and your cell will teach you everything.' What does this mean for a frantic world that cannot keep still and is constantly looking for the next thrill? Stability was prized by the early monastic communities for the simple reason that it forced a person to work out what it meant to follow Christ in this situation here and now and realise that it would not be easier/more comfortable/more successful somewhere else.

The devil appeared to a brother disguised as an angel of light and said to him, 'I am Gabriel and I have been sent to you.' The brother said to him, 'See, if it is not someone else to whom you have been sent; as for me, I am not worthy of it' – and immediately the devil vanished.[8]

One of the most intriguing and oft-repeated sayings is that of Abba Joseph who was visited by Abba Lot:

Abba Lot went to see Abba Joseph and said to him, 'Abba, as far as I can I say my little office, I fast a little, I pray and meditate, I live in peace and as far as I can, I purify my thoughts. What else can I do?' Then the old man stood up and stretched his hands towards heaven. His fingers became like ten lamps of fire and he said to him, 'If you will you can become all flame.'[9]

While the above sayings are all by Fathers, Sister Benedicta has been instrumental in pointing out that there were also Desert

Mothers, women who adopted the life and values of the desert. Her book *Harlots of the Desert* is subtitled *A study in repentance* and gives a window into the lives of these courageous women who sought God in prayer.

The goal of the monk was to be totally united with Christ in the power of the Spirit, to be aflame with the love of God. Many contemporary songs sung in churches today express that same desire. What the Desert Fathers and Mothers provide us with is a down-to-earth way of life that centres on humility and grace. Learning to see them in their own time and place and how that led to the things that concerned them, challenged them and ministered to them can help us in our own time to find practical paths towards holiness that bear witness to the life of God at work in us. The circumstances are vastly different; the vices and virtues that kept the monks grounded are not so different.

St Bede: father of English history

Sister Benedicta has written about many other characters from Church history, who, like the desert dwellers, have stores of wisdom that the Church continues to need today. One of the most exciting discoveries I made early on was the work of the Venerable Bede (AD 673–735), who lived his life from the age of seven as a monk in the north-east of England, not far from where I had been brought up.

Bede, known as the father of English History, recorded the story of the coming of Christianity to the British Isles. Through Bede's *Ecclesiastical History of the English People* I first came to know characters who have stayed with me all my life, challenging and inspiring me about my Christian witness and life of prayer: men and women such as Cuthbert, Aidan and Hild.

I gained some encouragement to keep on drawing on these great ancestors in the faith only recently by hearing Sister Benedicta's own story recounted on a visit to her at Fairacres in Oxford. She was brought up in the north-west of England, so she is a grammar-school girl, like me. As a teenager, I felt God had something he wanted me to do but I had no idea what it was. Sister Benedicta, however, was clear from an early age that God was calling her to be a nun. Like me, she read history at a northern university and was guided and influenced by a number of significant individuals to pursue her research in a particular direction. There the similarities end. She became a nun and a translator and historian, while I eventually was ordained and married.

St Anselm

Benedicta's first publication was *The Prayers and Meditations of St Anselm*, in 1973. How interesting that the current Archbishop of Canterbury launched a new religious community in 2015 at Lambeth called the Community of St Anselm. In an age that eschews institutional religion, there is still a hunger for God and the conviction that Christians from our past may have something to say that will help us. Designed for young people who are serious enough about God to consider giving up a year to pursue a deeper spiritual life, the experience is described as 'a transformative year of shared life, prayer, study and service'.[10]

The original Anselm (AD 1033–1109) was a scholar monk who became Archbishop of Canterbury. He was a man whose life as a monk was inseparable from his ideas and theology. His greatest philosophical work, *Proslogion*, is still studied and admired by theologians and philosophers today. Sister Benedicta included it whole in her *Prayers and Meditations*, believing it to be the best example of its own title 'faith seeking understanding' and therefore a prayer. For Anselm, as, I believe, for Sister Benedicta, prayer and thinking belong together. He sought to bring to bear all the powers of his mind upon what he already believed, claiming that it is impossible to prove the unknowable essence of God unless faith is part of the equation. 'Thank you good Lord,' he said, 'for by your gift I first believed and now by your illumination I understand.'[11]

Anselm sent copies of his prayers and meditations to friends who asked for them, along with simple, practical advice on how they could be used. He lived at a time of change in the way Christians prayed, for the eleventh century saw a move towards a more interior and personal mode of prayer. Anselm took the Psalms and crafted material to assist people who wanted to learn to pray this way. In an age where many are returning to liturgy in which the Psalms feature so prominently, perhaps reading Anselm with the help of a guide such as Sister Benedicta could help those who are longing to deepen their prayers. The personal in prayer is well established, but there is often a sense of wanting more depth. Anselm's practical advice to such people is simple: the first thing is to want to pray, and the second is to set time aside from concern with oneself in order to be 'free for a while for God'. His prayers and meditations were designed to help those who got this far and needed help and encouragement to persevere.

The window cleaner

Sister Benedicta's way is to allow the texts of the early Christians to speak for themselves, and she encourages her readers to do the same. In conversation she remarked that she sees herself as a window cleaner, an image she has also described in writing:

> [It is] for me like looking through windows of different coloured glass at many people, times and places; my task is that of a window-cleaner, making it possible for others both to see through clearly and pass over to find pasture, as I do, among such friends.[12]

A good example of her method is found in Chapter 6 of *High King of Heaven*, 'Anglo-Saxon prayers'. Two texts formed the basis for prayer among Anglo-Saxon Christians: the Psalms and the Lord's Prayer. Most of what is written is brief commentary on longer extracts from original sources. In a chapter of 19 pages, there is one extract compiled from Bede and Alcuin on the Lord's Prayer that runs to five pages (pp. 84–9). Prayer, for the Anglo-Saxons, comments Sister Benedicta, was linked with the Scriptures, especially, but not exclusively, with Psalms and with the Our Father.

Dying is a spiritual issue

Earlier in *High King of Heaven* it was noted that one of the attractions of Christianity for the Anglo-Saxons was its perspective of a wider reality which lay around their lives. Life on earth was the threshold of the kingdom of God.[13] As such it transformed attitudes to death and eternity. Is this something we have become immune to in the twenty-first century? Death is an affront, even to Christians, and our culture has done everything it can to hide it from our gaze. Not only are we reluctant to talk about it, but we have also hidden it from view, so that even funeral services may be conducted without a coffin present.

This is very different from the biblical and early Christian attitude where death is seen as the last enemy, yes, but at the same time it is the gateway into eternity and not something to be shunned. For the Anglo-Saxons, faith in Christ, the victor over death and hell, led to them seeing death as the beginning, not the end. It seems vital that we learn from these men and women how to talk about death in new ways that more closely reflect what we profess to believe and to approach our own death from the foundation of faith in the risen Christ. This is an underdeveloped aspect of spirituality in the postmodern world which often colludes with the reluctance to explore the resources provided by the Christian faith to help us face death and bereavement. Writers Ann Lewin and Margaret Guenther would agree with the Anglo-Saxons, as we have already seen. With this in mind, the last chapter of *High King of Heaven* is illuminating because it continues the story on to the terrible sacking of Lindisfarne by the Danes in AD 793. Of course, the Anglo-Saxons were not immune to suffering, and this was an extreme instance of what was all too often the reality of a life where there were no comforts to ease the agonies that suffering brought in its wake.

Sister Benedicta focuses on the place of the cross in Christian spirituality, and in doing so reminds us all that the cross is not something designed to make us 'feel better, nicer, more comfortable, more victorious, more reconciled to tragedy, better able to cope with life and death; it was rather the centre of the fire in which [we are] to be changed'.[14] Bede drew attention towards the end of his life to the slack and superficial nature of much of the Church's witness, and 50 years later, when the Danes came, it was found wanting. It was up to King Alfred the Great to foster a return to loving God and neighbour more seriously. Benedicta Ward concludes:

> In darkness, desolation and shame, in facing the poverty and weakness of the heart, there is the place of the Cross and of the light of life and redemption, because that is the place where God is and no other. If Christianity is true, the only success we know anything about is a man nailed to a cross and still with the Father.[15]

By 'still' here is meant stillness before God so that he may act.

Sister Benedicta freely acknowledges the encouragement of others on the direction of her work: academics, mentors and fellow religious. Their names read like a roll call of the history I studied at university, and to know that they had encouraged this woman to pursue study as part of her vocation added a new dimension to them in my mind. Some of them were members of religious orders themselves, and the theme of the love of learning and the desire for God going hand in hand characterizes her own life and work. It is also a reminder that she belonged to a generation of pioneering women scholars who had to work hard to gain recognition, no matter how brilliant their research. She is included in a collection of essays entitled *Women Medievalists and the Academy*.[16]

Sister Benedicta offers contemporary Christians a spirituality that is robust and real, the very opposite of what so many think of when they hear the word 'spirituality'. There is nothing private, consumerist or add-on to the Christianity of the likes of St Cuthbert, St Julian or John Bunyan. These characters wrestled with God and with the condition of the world in which they found themselves to press through to a relationship with God that was gained through self-knowledge and God-knowledge. Sister Benedicta emphasizes that they were human beings just like us, men and women who used their life experiences in conversation with Scripture to offer a vision through their writings of how the gospel brings the light that transforms everything.

Key themes
- Christian holiness
- Scholarship and prayer
- The Christian life in historical context
- The work of translation
- Saints for today
- The study of the Scriptures

Questions and action points
- 'Go to your cell and your cell will teach you everything.' How do you react to this statement? Do you have somewhere that could be a 'cell' where you find stillness with God? A room, a church, a favourite seat or park bench?

- Does the idea of being inspired by Christians from the past excite you or remind you of dismal history lessons at school? How could the concept of the communion of saints, the 'great . . . cloud of witnesses' referred to in Hebrews 12.1, make their witness more real for you?
- Is there any field of knowledge or a particular skill where you see yourself as a 'window-cleaner', making something accessible to others? Do you see this activity as part of what it means to be human, helping us to relate to one another, blessing one another and being an encouragement to expand our horizons?
- Men and women in late antiquity and the early medieval world were much more conscious of the fragility of life and the proximity of death. What resources do you rely on in the face of your own death and that of those dear to you? Does the understanding of the cross in your faith tradition help you here?
- Who has nurtured and encouraged you as you have chosen the pathways of your life's journey so far? Are there those whom you have influenced in turn? Is there anyone now who needs your encouragement?

Select writings and translations

Give Love and Receive the Kingdom (Brewster: Paraclete Press, 2018).
Harlots of the Desert: A study in repentance in early monastic sources (London: Mowbray, 1987).
High King of Heaven: Aspects of early English spirituality (London: Mowbray, 1999).
The Lives of the Desert Fathers, Norman Russell (trans.) with introduction by Benedicta Ward (London: Mowbray, 1980).
The Prayers and Meditations of St Anselm (London: Penguin, 1973).
The Sayings of the Desert Fathers. The Alphabet Collection (London: Mowbray (1975, 1981).
The Venerable Bede (London: Geoffrey Chapman, new edition, 1998).

The Wisdom of the Desert Fathers (Oxford: Fairacres Publications (1975, 1981).

Further reading

Jane Chance (ed.), *Women Medievalists and the Academy* (Madison: University of Wisconsin Press, 2005).

9

Marilynne Robinson:
the givenness of things

The attraction of a book with the title *When I Was a Child I Read Books* is irresistible to a bibliophile, for that is exactly what I remember most about my own childhood. That formative experience set me and so many others on a course that meant life must include reading at every convenient, and often inconvenient, moment.

Where my own reading was a mixture of classics and the ephemeral, however, Marilynne Robinson states at the outset of this essay that her reading was not indiscriminate. She preferred books that were 'old and thick and hard'.[1] To help her, she made vocabulary lists. Well, I liked books that were old and thick and hard too, but I read my fair share of Enid Blyton, and later Agatha Christie, alongside them, and I still enjoy the occasional easy read to lull me to sleep on a summer's day. I did not read Emily Dickinson as a child, as Marilynne did, but the Bible was certainly part of the staple diet at home.

Being a bookish child in the West of America made Marilynne Robinson unusual, and people commented, but it set the course of her life. She has lived a life made up of books because she is a lover of books: those she has written, those she has read and those she sees emerging from her writing classes.

Gilead

It seems safe to say that Marilynne Robinson's novel, *Gilead*, will endure and become a classic. In it, the Revd John Ames, an aged preacher with a weak heart, is writing to his young son, whom he knows he will not live to see to manhood. The setting is 1950s rural Iowa which borders Kansas, the scene of a great struggle between abolitionists and their opponents before the Civil War. Refuges were built to shelter escaping slaves in Iowa, close to the border with Kansas. Ames's grandfather had been involved in that struggle.

As Ames looks back on his own long life and the lives of his father and grandfather, we are given insights into the history of the USA through this one family. The tone of Ames's reminiscences as he wonders what God makes of his concerns and his self-justification is deliberately questioning, and this enables us to question them too. For me this is one of the most appealing aspects of Robinson's novels. The humility of John Ames frees me to read reflectively, without feeling that I am being manipulated into siding with this or that point of view. Choosing to make the main characters preachers enables the author to use religious language and themes and to address profound spiritual questions that affect us all. Ames, in particular, with his honesty and vulnerability, holds up a mirror to our own internal fears and prejudices.

Robinson once said that she sees fiction more like painting than reportage, which gives readers the freedom to imagine and make their own connections. *Gilead* has been described as a book that talks about religion to non-religious people in ways that resonate and indeed empower, because we feel as though we are being invited to play God – for example, in the choice of whether or not to forgive as Ames wrestles with his attitude towards his godson Jack.

C. S. Lewis, who was an expert in medieval English literature as well as a Christian apologist and novelist himself, wrote:

In reading great literature I become a thousand men [sic] and yet remain myself. Like the night sky in the Greek poem I see with a myriad eyes, but it is still I who see. Here, as in worship, in love, in moral action, and in knowing, I transcend myself; and am never more myself than when I do.[2]

Novels and theology

As someone who has often found more theology in novels than in many theology textbooks, I have had many conversations about what exactly novels have to teach us about spirituality. There is research, for example, that claims that people who read have more empathy. Literary fiction trains the emotions, requiring the reader to infer, predict, interpret and evaluate. Like our muscles, our emotions need exercise to mature.

Good writing shows us that human beings are complex creatures, and this comes across in Marilynne Robinson's novels with great force. A professing Christian and an academic with a powerful intellect, she teaches literature and creative writing along with theology, but her widest audience is the readers of her novels. As well as being a storyteller, she is an essayist, and her non-fiction writing explores the world of ideas, including the Calvinism that influences her thinking. In a review of *The Givenness of Things*, she spoke about the process of writing a novel and how it comes to birth:

> I feel a novel begin to cohere in my mind before I know much more about it than that it has the heft of a long narrative. This heft is a physical sensation. A forming novel is a dense atmosphere more than it is a concept or an idea. I find my way into it by finding a voice that can tell it and then it unfolds within the constraints of its own nature, which seems arbitrary to me but is inviolable by me.[3]

Marilynne Robinson's titles are deeply evocative: *Gilead*, *Home*, *When I Was a Child I Read Books*, to name three of them. Gilead is a biblical place name, and in both Hebrew and Aramaic it means 'heap [of stones] of testimony' (Genesis 31.47–48). The area, which is east of the River Jordan, was abundant in aromatic spices and gums, giving rise to the lament in Jeremiah the prophet, 'Is there no balm in Gilead?' (Jeremiah 8.22).

Gilead may be a small, insignificant town, but it is the arena where great and universal themes of love, memory, forgiveness and grace are played out. To John Ames, the very insignificance of the place has a Christlike quality about it: it seems that the town looks like 'whatever hope becomes after it begins to weary a little, then weary a little more'.[4] He muses at the end of the story that he is content to be buried there until the 'great and general incandescence'.[5] Like all classic novels, *Gilead* is a book to return to in the expectation that it has yet more to reveal in its narrative and characters and their reflections, particularly in this case the old preacher, John Ames.

Home

The word 'home' evokes powerful feelings for almost every human being, from serene and lasting happiness to memories of misery and loss. Robinson's novel of that name explores the same town of Gilead, turning to Ames's great friend and fellow preacher, John Boughton, and his relationship with his wayward son Jack.

Jack is named after John Ames and is his godson. Jack is in trouble from childhood on, and *Home* is the story of his homecoming and efforts to make peace with his troubled past. His sister Glory has also come home to Gilead, and the relationships in the family and with John Ames form the core of this novel.

Home explores the issues of why Jack has turned out the way he has, despite being showered with love and care. Jack himself cannot explain this and is unable to show intimacy with anyone else. Yet there is something lovable about his character that invites us to refuse simplistic definitions of good and bad. In one scene at Jack's home in the kitchen, during the baking of some pies, his father is reminiscing about his grandmother's habits. Jack leans against the counter with a wistful smile, thinking of the disappointment he thought he knew in his father, when the latter looked at him. All the father said, however, was, 'It's a powerful thing family,' and then, 'Well, at least you're home.'[6]

Lila

I found the third novel in this trilogy the most arresting. *Lila* is really a prequel to *Gilead* (although each novel also stands alone) and is about the young woman whom Ames married in his old age and who has been on the periphery of the two previous books, both in terms of the stories they tell and of the conversations recorded. She has an unexplained past which is utterly different from that of Ames or anyone else in *Gilead*. In *Lila* we discover what that past was like for her and how it shaped her outlook on the world. It tells how, as a mistreated infant in a violent household, she is taken, maybe stolen, by Doll, a rough vagabond woman who cares for her and how together they struggle to survive along with a group of wandering farm workers. Eventually the group falls victim to the Great Depression and the grinding poverty of the dustbowls of America. Lila spends time in a whorehouse before she ends up in Gilead and meets the Revd Ames.

What an unlikely match this is. She is a wonderful foil for Ames in every way: young (though old in the way life has treated her), powerful and angry, with a lifetime of suffering and hardship. She interrogates his unshakeable faith with her sceptical approach to God and religion. While Ames is constantly reflecting on theological questions, Lila says, 'I don't understand theology. I don't think I like it. Lots of folk live and die and never worry themselves about it.'[7]

We learn to see the world through Lila's eyes. There are no chapters and the story reads as if we are privy to Lila's thought world.

Her inner conflict – whether she should go, or whether she should stay – her fear of commitment and inability to trust anyone, Ames included, and her inner voice telling her to look out for herself since no one else would, all moved me greatly.

Where is wisdom found?

Lila is a strong character, fiercely loyal to Doll and the other wandering labourers. In a similar way, Ames's generosity, his gentleness and compassion, his willingness to admit that he doesn't know so many things with any certainty, his devotion to Lila even though it might cost him dearly, and his accumulated wisdom through his faithful preaching and pastoral work make him an attractive character to ponder. There are many questions raised here that humans have always asked and will continue to do so: Does prayer work? Are we just the products of our upbringing? How can we forgive ourselves? How may we deal with shame? to name just a few.

The Bible features prominently in the story, as both Lila and Ames read it and reflect on what they find there. Lila reads avidly, loving its wild and strange language that speaks to her, even though she does not often understand it. This raises interesting questions about language and understanding. Does it matter that we do not always understand all the words in what we read, especially in church? Do we overcompensate and end up dumbing down and emptying out the mystery of God and faith by over-explaining? Kathleen Norris wrote *Amazing Grace* to unpack religious jargon, but is *Lila* presenting us with the other side of the coin?

The novel is shot through with grace, and there is an underlying debate about whether God can let go of any creature he has made and whom he loves. This is brilliantly depicted in a scene where Lila tries to 'wash off' her baptism, having realized that it cuts her off from Doll and the others with whom she has shared so much. It is poignant, too, that she came to this realization by overhearing Ames and Boughton coolly discussing the eternal fate of unbelievers and she realized that such a one was Doll.

The novel does not answer the question for us. As with all great stories, it raises the question and invites us to make our own response. At one point Lila says, 'I have been wondering lately why things happen the way they do,' and Ames replies, 'I've been wondering about that more or less the whole of my life.'[8]

The point of existence – a word Lila learned from Ames but knows a great deal about anyway – is explored throughout the novel. The honesty of Ames in trying to answer Lila's questions without being glib is both a winsome feature of his character and a wonderful way to open up the same issues for the reader to ponder. There is humour in the book too, such as the baptism scene and the way Lila brings Ames down to earth when he is theologizing. At one point, when Ames is quoting Calvin again, she says, 'I didn't even know he was dead. Calvin. The way you and Boughton talk about him.'[9]

Housekeeping

Perhaps the least well-known novel by Marilynne Robinson is her first: *Housekeeping*. It is unrelated to the three that came afterwards and was published in 1980, so there was a long gap before another novel emerged from her pen.

Housekeeping is the story of two sisters: Ruth, who is the narrator, and Lucille, who are passed between relatives after the suicide of their mother. Eventually they come to be with their transient aunt Sylvie. The book explores how each of the three is changed by living with the others. In *When I Was a Child I Read Books*, Robinson says that *Housekeeping* was meant as a sort of demonstration of the intellectual culture of her childhood.[10] The narrator of the story, Ruth, makes only the allusions that were available to Marilynne herself at that age.

It is in this book that the author experiments with metaphor, which she had begun to do while studying for her doctorate. As a writer she says that she continuously attempts to make inroads on the vast terrain of what *cannot* be said, at least by her.[11] We are being invited to reflect on words in Marilynne's writing as well as immerse ourselves in a story. It is the same in *Gilead*, where John Ames confesses that he believes deeply but cannot put into words exactly what it is that he believes. There comes a point when words are simply inadequate, yet writers like Marilynne Robinson go far in helping us to articulate those profound and elusive ideas that we grasp at with our intellects. She writes about her use of metaphor to render the world comprehensible. She refers to *Housekeeping* as a very allusive book, for example, because the narrator deploys every resource she has to try to make the world comprehensible.

Choices

At the end of the day, *Gilead* remains my favourite Robinson novel and it is the one I read again and again, always finding something new. It has an elegiac feel, and I can almost hear the old preacher talking to his son through his letter. I would love to have listened to him preach, especially his sermon on Hagar and Ishmael when, to his horror, his friend Boughton's wayward son turns up to church that very day, as Ames tries to express his thoughts on providence.[12] He sees similarities with the story of Abraham and Isaac, commenting that, 'Great faith is required to give the child up, trusting God to honour the parents' love for him by assuring that there will indeed be angels in that wilderness.'[13] He remains dissatisfied with his sermon, noting that it was such a difficult question to raise at all, but he did so because he is asked about it so often, and even so he has never yet explained it to his own satisfaction.

The inadequacy of words is a recurring theme for this preacher and husband of a woman bathed in mystery, for Ames is acutely conscious that although his faith means everything to him, he is unable to explain it properly in words. On this occasion the presence of Jack, who has been a thorn in Ames's side all his life, adds to his difficulties by distracting him, but the question of God's providence keeps on surfacing throughout the novel. He ponders the idea that in every encounter with another human being it is as if a question were being asked: 'What is the Lord asking of me in this moment, in this situation?' There is freedom to act in the appropriate way or not, but an invitation is offered to demonstrate that in some small way we participate in the grace that saves us. You are 'free to act by your own lights'. And he also notes that:

> Calvin says somewhere that each of us is an actor on a stage and God is the audience. That metaphor has always interested me, because it makes us artists of our behaviour, and the reaction of God to us might be thought of as aesthetic rather than morally judgmental in the ordinary sense.[14]

Forgiveness

Ames admits that his sense of Christian forbearance has masked his dislike of his godson Jack, but things come to a head when Jack allows Ames to bless him. The old man realizes that this young man has received nothing but love but has given nothing back, and yet he shows that he is in fact capable of love after all. Ames's belief that every human being is made in the image of God and has something lovable about them is thus vindicated by this event.

There are many little asides in the novel that demand pause for consideration. Ames recalls a dream in which his mother came into his room and sat in a chair in the corner and stayed there, very still and calm. It made him feel wonderfully safe, wonderfully happy. When he awoke she was indeed present. He remarks, 'I have that same feeling in the church, that I am dreaming what is true.'[15]

Robinson herself goes to church because in childhood she realized that this was the only place that took seriously the sense of wonder before life. Here is another fascinating aspect of this writer that surprises. So many people today have abandoned churchgoing, offering as reasons boredom, irrelevance or infantile approaches to the world. Church is often the last place anyone would think of looking to satisfy their spiritual hunger. Why is this so?

Faith, values and culture

Marilynne Robinson is an able and eloquent defender of the Christian faith. Indeed, she has been described as someone who can make Christianity 'something that an intelligent and sensitive adult need not be ashamed to think and feel with – even to inhabit with her own solidity of commitment'.[16] Her essays frequently take up the theme of religion. *Absence of Mind: The dispelling of inwardness from the modern myth of the self* (2010), for example, evolved from a series of lectures she gave at Yale University in 2009 addressing the debate between science and religion. The discussion continued in *When I Was a Child I Read Books* (2012) and *The Givenness of Things* (2015), along with politics and culture.

Marilynne has spent most of her life studying American history and literature and admires American laws and institutions, its poetry and philosophy. But she observes that the language of public life has lost the character of generosity and the largeness of spirit that created and supported the best of American institutions and brought reform to the worst of them. She believes they have been erased from historical memory.[17] She sees the reason for this to be an understanding of capitalism on all sides as grasping materialism that is damaging to democracy. She is critical of Christian solutions that are simplistic and watered-down versions of the real thing, while insisting that Christian faith can help us face the deepest questions of our age in a way that is clear and takes seriously the mystery that is life.

She believes that the thinker who can help us here is John Calvin. One person I have spoken to who heard her speak at the Albert Hall in London heard her tell the crowded auditorium that we should all be reading Calvin, though perhaps not uncritically, since she poses some interesting questions in her books about the theology that is associated with his name.

The world is a wonderful place

Marilynne Robinson's essays and novels make it clear that she sees all of life as a unity and the world as a splendid and wonderful place. One of the questions that interests Marilynne in her writings is why we seem to be so easily distracted from what is good in life. This is a deeply spiritual question, especially for a distracted culture like our own. Life, to Robinson, is a mystery, and a beautiful one at that. Her writing is pervaded by a sense of astonishment before life, rather like the nineteenth-century poet Emily Dickinson. She is also full of wonder at the way human beings are capable of exploring this astonishing world and reflecting on its meaning.

She writes about the soul and what it is. For contemporary writers on spirituality, this is a vexed question, for the concept of the soul is encumbered with so many unhelpful associations today. For Marilynne, the soul is the experience of selfhood and it is interesting, complex and beautiful. In an interview with Krista Tippett for the podcast 'On being' in 2012, entitled 'The mystery we are', Robinson reflected on the relationship between science and faith, rejecting as too simplistic a straight either/or approach. The world, she remarked, is always more than we can see or measure and the mystery of nature has always been the driving force behind scientific research.[18]

Her most recent collection of essays, *What Are We Doing Here?*, often quotes another dead theologian, this time the great eighteenth-century American Puritan, Jonathan Edwards. He proclaimed that 'Nature is God's greatest evangelist',[19] a tenet that would be applauded by many of the writers represented in this book. So what does nature tell us about God? asks Marilynne, emphasizing awe and wonder, mystery and sheer astonishment at the world. She points to recent discoveries in astronomy and physics to argue her case against the so-called 'new atheism' and is highly critical of what she terms 'the materialist approach to reality'. As in *When I Was a Child I Read Books*, unbridled capitalism comes under ferocious attack. The world is full of mystery and there is so much that we do not know. One of the essays focuses on the theological virtues of faith, hope and love, while another on 'slander' shows that words are not neutral or harmless. They can achieve great good but also great evil.

Robinson has received numerous prestigious literary awards for her books, including the Pulitzer Prize and the National Book Critics Circle Award for fiction for *Gilead*, the Orange Prize (later Baileys Women's Prize for Fiction) for *Home* and the National Book Critics Circle Award for *Lila*. *Housekeeping* won the Hemingway Foundation/PEN Award for best first novel as well as being nominated for the Pulitzer Prize. In 2014 Robinson was awarded the National Humanities Medal for her 'grace and intelligence in writing'. Read her for yourself and discover these qualities, and more.

Key themes

- Awe and astonishment before life
- The mystery and unique worth of every human being
- The ability of Christian faith to address the deepest questions of our time
- The importance of trusting God's purpose for humanity and living it out amid all the ambiguity of life
- Great admiration for the theologian John Calvin
- The power of stories
- Words and what they can and cannot say

- What it means to be human and in relationship with others

Questions and action points

- Which novels have you read that help you address key questions about life and meaning?
- If you have read any of Marilynne Robinson's novels, what is it about them that makes them stand out for you?
- Have you read any other novels where religion is the focus of attention in an open and interesting way?
- *Lila* is dedicated 'to Iowa'. What novels have you read where the landscape is key to the story?
- What are your thoughts on growing old? If you have read *Gilead*, *Home* and/or *Lila*, are there passages that have helped you reflect on ageing?
- *Lila* speaks of the 'wildness' of the Bible. Do we try too hard to tame it? How do we do this? What parts do you avoid reading and why?
- Do something that brings you face to face with the splendour and wonder of the world.
- Do you share the author's amazement at the way human beings are capable of exploring the world and reflecting on its meaning?

Select writings

Absence of Mind: The dispelling of inwardness from the modern myth of the self (New Haven: Yale, 2010).

Gilead (New York: Farrar, Straus and Giroux, 2004; London: Virago, 2005).

The Givenness of Things (London: Virago, 2015).

Home (New York: Farrar, Straus and Giroux, 2008; London: Virago, 2008).

Housekeeping (New York: Farrar, Straus and Giroux, 1980; London: Faber and Faber, 1981).

Lila (New York: Farrar, Straus and Giroux, 2004; London: Virago, 2014).

What Are We Doing Here? (London: Virago, 2018).

When I Was a Child I Read Books (London: Virago, 2012).

10

Barbara Brown Taylor: struggles with the Church

Reading sermons is something of a niche activity, even among enthusiastic supporters of preaching and its role. After all, a sermon is an event, and one that is primarily to do with hearing. Not many sermons translate to the page effectively, for, as Barbara Brown Taylor observes, it can sometimes be no more than a 'rumour' of what the sermon was really about.[1] There are notable exceptions, which continue to be read as literary gems as well as for their striking content. In my view, it always helps to know something about the preacher. Lancelot Andrewes, for example, was a master of words and images, while Martin Luther had such fire in his bones that he set the whole of Europe alight.

The art of preaching

Some preachers have written about the art of preaching itself, and Barbara Brown Taylor is one of those. She is a well-known preacher in the USA, and her books (she is a prolific writer) are less collections of sermons than the translation of spirituality into everyday life. The first one I read was *An Altar in the World*, which was written out of the conviction that we do not have to go on long journeys to find God, for he is right there beneath our feet. Barbara shares the astonishment experienced by Marilynne Robinson and explored in the previous chapter, in the face of this wonderful world.

The thesis of *An Altar in the World* is that there is no way to God apart from real life in the real world. Each chapter begins with the phrase 'The practice of . . .' and includes such activities as waking up, getting lost, walking the earth and saying no. Each named practice has a subtitle that may or may not sound directly religious in tone. Thus 'The practice of saying no' is subtitled 'Sabbath', while 'The practice of walking the earth' is subtitled 'Groundedness'.

I was specially struck by the chapter called 'The practice of paying attention', subtitled 'Reverence'. A religious sounding word, reverence could be taken out of its churchy setting as long as it were reserved for reverencing pretty things such as sunsets and other people like us, but Barbara Brown Taylor is not letting us off the hook as easily as that. She describes moving to the country, close to where chickens were reared en masse for food. Driving behind a truck tightly packed with chickens on the way to slaughter and seeing them huddled and unprotected inside while their feathers glanced off her windscreen opened her eyes to something sacramental. She saw what had to die so that she could live, and while she did not become a vegetarian, she remarked that from then on she cooked her chicken with 'unprecedented reverence'.[2]

Altars in the world

Finding God in the world is a theme common to a number of the writers represented here, but it was Barbara's personal story that led me to include her. Ordained to a highly successful ministry, she left it to become a college teacher. She wrote about that experience in *Leaving Church*. Yet in 2014 Barbara Brown Taylor was named as one of the world's 100 most influential people. Why? Could it be that she has struck a chord with the many people who are leaving church but not losing faith in North America, where her influence is greatest?

Something in her convictions and expressed in her writing resonates with people, causing them to buy her books and listen to her at her public speaking engagements. Many of her books have won awards. She writes with conviction and she does not pull her punches. She is often critical of the Church of which she is a part, but that is because she wants us to break out of our churchiness and discover God 24/7.

Reflecting on the story of Jacob, who dreamed he saw a ladder reaching to heaven in a barren place he named Bethel, she comments, 'Earth is so thick with divine possibility that it is a wonder that we can walk anywhere without cracking our shins on altars.'[3] If you are someone who is weary of crossing one day off the calendar with no sense of what makes the last day different from the next, then *An Altar in the World* could help you to wake up to the holy under your feet.

A writer in earnest

Barbara's writing is vivid; the metaphors and quips follow on one after the other with breathless speed. At first sight she can sound flippant, but she is in deadly earnest to get the message across that God is so much bigger than the churches in which we try to contain him. A theological educator, Barbara wears her theological skill and knowledge lightly. Indeed, she is adamant that theology must penetrate beyond the intellect and affect what we do if it is to be real. She often refers to characters from the history of the Church without making readers feel they are ignorant or that they are being instructed. Church Fathers, reformers, saints and preachers are mentioned to tell a story, illustrate a point or embed a truth that we may have forgotten about.

I like the way she weaves stories of her childhood in and out of her sermons in *The Preaching Life*, or describes her relationship with the dark in *Learning to Walk in the Dark*. She was brought up on a farm in rural Kansas, USA, and this shaped her as a person. She grew up at a time when most people took religion for granted and went to church. Her observation is that when she was at primary school, everybody attended church and followed the rules of a Christian lifestyle, but by the time she got to secondary school, this era had passed and disillusionment had set in.

In the first sermon in *The Preaching Life* she explores what that disillusionment feels and looks like and notes that it means the loss of illusion, in this case about God, the world and ourselves. Thus it is not a bad thing to 'lose the lies we have mistaken for the truth'.[4] For some, herself included, there is a way back, as curtain after curtain is drawn back to show that the failure is not God's but our own. We slowly discover that God is 'greater than our imagination, wiser than our wisdom, more dazzling than the universe, as present as the air I breathe and utterly beyond my control'.[5] For Barbara Brown Taylor, what makes her a Christian is that in Jesus Christ she found a 'mediator, an advocate, a flesh and blood handle on the inscrutable mystery that gives birth to everything that is'.[6]

Relational spirituality

Barbara Brown Taylor is unashamedly relational in the way that she writes, weaving her life in and out of her material. This bears out her contention that being relational is fundamental to being human and I suspect contributes greatly to her popularity. Barbara writes fluently about how she found her way into the Episcopalian Church from a home where her dad was Roman Catholic and her mum Methodist, and churchgoing was spasmodic. What drew her was a mixture of 'liturgy, tradition, tolerance, transcendence, communion'.[7]

This got me pondering about what had drawn me at the age of 21 from a strong Nonconformist tradition to the Anglican Church. I expected a different list, but in fact it came out the same. Liturgy was the first draw. The words repeated day by day, week by week, and a love of the focus on communion. Tradition certainly, as I made the transition while studying the English Reformation and the formation of the Church of England, which refused to let go of its long and valuable history. Tolerance was a surprise at first, until I remembered that asking questions was regarded as having an inquiring mind rather than being out of order. It had been my guilty secret to love mystery and words like 'ineffable', along with concepts like the poetic imagination and spiritual yearning. Communion with God and with one another, a sense of the communion of saints past as well as present and all held within the invitation to the heavenly banquet which we celebrate each time we come to the Lord's table.

What Barbara wanted more than anything was intimacy with God. The tragedy of her energetic and successful ministry was that she discovered that this was the one thing she had lost. Given that she worked up to 80 hours a week and learned to live permanently 'right on the edge of panic', she had no space left to foster her relationship with God.[8] She had to leave ministry to learn to be human.

Leaving church to find God

Leaving Church is a book all clergy should read, but it has things to say to the rest of the Church too. Barbara writes about the expectations that are loaded on to anyone with a dog collar, how she was never off duty and always expected to be OK. She reflects on the power the role gives to clergy and what happened to her when she took her collar off. She lost much and especially missed celebrating Holy Communion with her congregation. But the gains, though painfully made, far outstripped the losses. Above all, she rediscovered her priesthood without the props. It was emptied out into the world as she gradually remembered that the Church is not a stopping place but a starting place for discerning God's presence in the world.[9]

Reflecting on the way the Church had shaped the totality of her reality, she wryly comments that even her junk mail was Christian. I believe many clergy and church leaders will relate to this. Like Barbara, one of my secret hopes in being ordained was that it would keep me close to God. Like her, I became very attached to the role, and it was only when I gave it up that I had my eyes and ears opened to a far bigger God than I had previously countenanced. Like Barbara, I had to learn that the call to serve God in whatever capacity is first and foremost the call to be fully human. This is what we are for. This is the heart of the incarnation.

Spirituality, as we have seen, is fundamentally relational to Barbara. She was willing to take the risk of losing certainty in order to recover the kind of faith that is built on trusting God to catch her even when she was not sure of anything.[10] In one of her sermons on Matthew in *The Gate of Heaven*, she brings this experience vividly to life. Describing the story of Peter attempting to walk on the water towards Jesus and failing, she asks, what if Peter had not sunk? Well, then it would no longer be a story about us. Most of us wish we had more faith, but we are afraid to let go and let God care for us. Like Peter, we doubt because we are afraid, because bad things happen, because life is so far beyond our control. Even when we hear Jesus say, 'Do not be afraid,' we find ourselves trusting and fearful at the same time, walking and sinking, believing and doubting. Faith and doubt coexist, and that is why we need Jesus. Christ returned with Peter to the boat, knowing that the only reason he was in the boat in the first place was that he wanted to have faith to follow his Lord.[11]

Wrestling with the word

Like Kathleen Norris, Barbara reflects on what the Bible is and is not. She does so in personal terms, describing how it has had an impact on her own experience. She calls it a 'field guide' to the divine presence in the world. Her statements in *The Preaching Life* are confident ones that bear witness to a life of wrestling with it in all its difficult parts as well as the comforting passages we all return to again and again. She says her relationship with the Bible is more like a marriage than a romance, which involves work in the same way:

Living with the text day in and day out, by listening to it and talking back to it, by making sure that I know what is behind the words it speaks to me and being certain I have heard it properly, by refusing to distance myself from the parts of it I do not like or understand, by letting my love for it show up in the everyday acts of my life.[12]

The Bible turned out to be not a fossil under glass but a thousand different things – a mirror, a scythe, a hammock, a lantern, a pair of binoculars, a high diving board, a bridge, a goad.[13]

Words are important to Barbara, and her own favourite of all the books she has written is one about words: *When God Is Silent: Divine language beyond words*. Its original title was *Famine in the Land: Homiletic restraint and the silence of God*, a reference to Amos 8. Barbara is suspicious of words, or at least words that are used to fill the silence when we have nothing of worth to say. We have to run out of words and let God be God.

There is an echo of John Ames, Marilynne Robinson's old preacher in *Gilead*, here. Barbara reflects at length on God's silence in the Bible, noticing that it often seems as though God is playing hide and seek with his people. Why would God, the Word of life, not speak? Her answer is that silence is God's final defence against our idolatry.[14] Some surprising things emerge when we consider God's silences in Scripture. Silence can be fearful, but it may be the herald of new life also. It is significant to remember that John the Baptist punctured the long silence of the desert to proclaim the approach of the kingdom of God.

The last chapter of *When God Is Silent* considers the place of economy of words, courtesy in speech and reverence in the language we choose. Less is more, and in times of famine we need simple fare, not junk food. While this is directed at preachers, there are things for all of us to attend to in a world where words are cheap and overworked.

Sermons

The second half of *The Preaching Life* consists of Barbara's sermons on various texts from the Bible. In the first she looks at our illusion of control through the story of the healing of Jairus' daughter. Her gift of relating Bible text to real life comes through very clearly here. Some sermons simply tell us to try harder or believe more strongly, while others never address the discrepancy between what happens in the Bible story and the experience of most people most of the time. In the stories, people seem to call on Jesus and get what they want. After all, Jairus' daughter was raised from the dead. Why doesn't the same thing happen to us when we ask Jesus for something? Do we not have enough faith? Did we get something wrong? No, says Barbara. That approach would just be another way of getting back control over our lives and God would be our puppet. She points out that the stories are not about us persuading God to do what we want at all. They are about who God is and how God acts and what God is like.[15] Her sermons show a close attention to the actual words of the text. She comments over and over again, 'There is a lot going on here.'

Barbara Brown Taylor is interested in what Christians do as much as, if not more than, what they profess to believe. The physicality of Christian faith permeates her writing. Whether she is describing our relationship with our bodies or advocating hard work as a spiritual practice, Barbara's spirituality is always earthed in the physical realm. In *An Altar in the World* there is a chapter called 'The practice of carrying water. Physical labour', which begins by describing an ice storm which trapped her and her husband, leaving them without power for four days, in language that reads like a thriller unfolding. She had to work extremely hard to keep the two of them and their livestock warm and fed.

She then talks about choosing work and learning to see our relationship with the earth differently. Digging potatoes is her example of work, and it lends itself perfectly to considering that we are dust and to dust we shall return (Genesis 3.19), but cleaning toilets also has lessons to teach. She makes much of the word 'adam' used to describe the first human created by God from the earth: *adamah*. The created being means 'earthling', and the first thing God did was to create a garden and put the earthling in it to till it and keep it. Keeping the earth is hard work, and it reminds us where we came from. It keeps us grounded. Work, she writes, offers us the chance to 'bear the reality of the universe in your flesh like a thorn'.[16]

Learning to Walk in the Dark

Learning to Walk in the Dark was written for three groups of people: young people, for whom their parents' faith does not resonate; people in midlife who have taken some knocks, including in the area of faith; and older people, such as the author, for whom dying draws closer and who need help to get ready.

Barbara left the Church altogether for a while, mainly because she could not countenance the dualistic divide of so much Christian teaching – good/evil, church/world, spirit/flesh, sacred/profane, light/dark – and this book is based on discovering the wisdom of accepting the unknown. It requires us to give up trying to be in control, to be prepared to take some knocks at first and finally to ask the darkness to teach us what we need to know.[17]

This all reminds me of Job and his story of learning to trust God in the darkness of his experience. Barbara calls this approach to faith 'lunar spirituality', since it follows the phases of the moon which waxes and wanes, mimicking life for the majority of us. She mentions this image of the spiritual life in *Leaving Church*, where she wrote about the need for church leaders always to be OK. This is 'solar spirituality', the sun always shining and the person's relationship with God on fire. But life is not like that for clergy any more than it is for the rest of us who call ourselves followers of Jesus. So her exploration of darkness here elaborates on what may happen to anyone. She embarked on a project with a great deal of fieldwork to expose her to darkness in many different areas of life, including recalling childhood fears, visiting underground caves and an experience of living as a blind person. She also draws on writers such as Thomas Merton, Julian of Norwich and John of the Cross, the latter especially familiar through his writings on darkness and the 'dark night of the soul'. The book contains themes that could be helpful to anyone struggling with the Church but continues to wrestle with Christian belief and experience. It could also help the many church leaders who feel under pressure to perform 24/7.

Key themes

- Being human
- Darkness
- Preaching
- Words
- Faith

Questions and action points

- Have you ever been made aware that the God you worship is loaded with false expectations? How do we make God in our own image?
- Can you recall any experience you had as a child that you later came to see as having deep spiritual significance? Can you describe the experience and the feelings you associate with it? What evokes longing in you?
- A field guide is a book designed to go in the pocket and be taken outside to aid identification of life and objects in the outdoors. Is this a helpful way for you to think about how the Bible applies to your life?
- 'The Bible turned out to be not a fossil under glass but a thousand different things – a mirror, a scythe, a hammock, a lantern, a pair of binoculars, a high diving board, a bridge, a goad'. Which of

these images expresses how you have encountered the Bible? Are there any other images that you would add?

- How helpful do you find the author's descriptions of 'solar spirituality' and 'lunar spirituality'?
- How do you keep your faith grounded in the way the author describes?

Select writings

An Altar in the World: Finding the sacred beneath our feet (Norwich: Canterbury Press, 2009).

The Gate of Heaven: Preaching Matthew (Norwich: Canterbury Press, 2004, 2016).

Learning to Walk in the Dark (Norwich: Canterbury Press, 2014, 2015).

Leaving Church: A memoir of faith (Norwich: Canterbury Press, 2006).

The Preaching Life: Living out your vocation (Cambridge, MA: Cowley Publications, 1993).

Speaking of Sin: The lost language of salvation (Norwich: Canterbury Press, 2000).

When God Is Silent: Divine language beyond words (Norwich: Canterbury Press, 1996).

11

Anne Lamott:
life in forgiveness school

I have lost count of the number of times I have recounted the story Anne Lamott tells of when her older brother, who was ten, was trying to write up a report for school that he had been given three months to complete. It was due in the next day. As he sat at the kitchen table close to tears, surrounded by paper, binders, pencils and unopened books on birds and paralysed by the enormity of the task, his father put his arm around the boy's shoulder and said, 'Bird by bird, buddy. Just take it bird by bird.' She gives her book on the writer's world and its pitfalls the title *Bird by Bird*.

Real-life faith

Anne Lamott is a quirky writer with an enormous sense of fun which she ably expresses in writing. *Christianity Today* magazine called her 'the funny, nutty, fast-talking born-again author'.[1] You can also listen to her self-deprecating TED talk on 'Twelve truths I have learned from life and writing'.

It is because her humour is self-effacing and her writing very honest that she has such wide appeal, I believe. She certainly has a readership that includes people of no faith as well as believers. She came to a faith in God against all the odds and then came to have confidence in herself. It is in the sharing of her personal struggles that her vulnerability is made plain and, far from being cringe-worthy or off-putting, it enables others to realize that all of us have fears and failures hidden away and are in need of healing.

She does not try to offer any easy answers to the paradox that is life, and her own experience is a prime example: 'My coming to faith did not start with a leap but rather a series of staggers.'[2] She calls earth 'forgiveness school' and likens grace to spiritual WD-40. It is with metaphors like these that faith becomes real and plausible to the modern world that is now so disconnected from the traditional language of religion. It is no surprise to learn that Anne Lamott is known as 'the people's writer', an epithet that is reinforced by her following on Facebook and Twitter, and the film that director Freida Lee Mock made about her life in 1999, *Bird by Bird with Annie: A film portrait of writer Anne Lamott.*

Anne Lamott's style reminds me of Margery Kempe, the fourteenth-century mystic, wife and mother who wrote non-intellectual prose about her experiences: her feelings, her reassurances from God about her worth, her involvement with the theological conversations of the day. The notion of the 'authority of experience' was a central current in feminist theory in the 1970s, which was built out of the personal and subjective witness of 'I'. Margery Kempe was formerly compared unfavourably with Julian of Norwich, her contemporary, for being too subjective, too emotional. Today, however, she is a crucial voice for historians attempting to access what ordinary people actually experienced in that period of history.

Experiencing grace

Anne has written fiction and non-fiction and has a prolific output. Only a selection is represented here. Her first novel, *Hard Laughter*, was written in 1980 when her father was dying of cancer. In 1993 she wrote a memoir called *Operating Instructions: A journal of my son's first year.* The titles of her books on faith suggest that she is not going to preach at us. They include *Grace (Eventually): Thoughts on faith, Traveling Mercies: Some thoughts on faith, Plan B: Further thoughts on faith* and *Help, Thanks, Wow.* In 1998 she received a Guggenheim Fellowship and in 2010 she was inducted into the California Hall of Fame. She continues to have a wide and enthusiastic following.

Grace (Eventually) is a sort of primer on faith and is poignant as well as funny in the way Anne looks at life. She describes her own search as a young woman who by the age of 21 had realized that almost everyone was struggling to wake up, to be loved and not to feel afraid all the time. That's what the cars, degrees, booze and drugs were about.[3]

Anne's early life was, by her own account, a mess, and all the time she knew she was looking for something. She used alcohol in particular to cope, and it was a long time after her initial spiritual awakening that she became free of her addiction. She tells the story with humour but it is painful to read all the same.[4] Each chapter of *Grace (Eventually)* stands alone and tells a story, usually against herself, in order to illustrate an aspect of God's grace.

Anne is grateful that there are no live feeds of our minds streaming online, but she reveals a good deal about her thought life in her writing. In one chapter, 'The muddling glory of God', she describes the process by which her ten-year-old son Sam learned to overcome his fear of sleeping alone in the dark. It was a long, slow process which began by sleeping on the floor next to his mother's bed until, bit by bit, he migrated through the house towards his own bed. 'That's me,' Anne remarks, as she tries to make any progress at all with family, in work, relationships, self-image:

scootch, scootch, stall; scootch, stall, catastrophic reversal; bog, bog, scootch. I wish grace and healing were more abracadabra kinds of things; also that delicate silver bells would ring to announce grace's arrival. But no, it's clog and slog and scootch, on the floor, in silence, in the dark.[5]

Anne writes in the same chapter about a bout of binge-eating. Her self-disgust is palpable, even though dressed up in humour. The story does not end with a great victory over her issues with food, but the recognition of grace and where it was revealed on that occasion gives a realistic and a hopeful message to anyone willing to listen.

Grace is fundamental to the Christian life, and unless we learn to recognize it, embrace it, rely on it and rejoice in it, we will miss the whole point of being alive. There are many discussions of grace in the abstract, but it is the daily experience of grace that brings it alive, and so to have a writer who can teach us where to look for it in the midst of our muddles, questions and multiple overwhelmings is a wonderful gift. If you have ever sent an email late at night and lived to regret it bitterly, struggled with bringing up a teenager, battled with resentment towards parental failings or fought with yourself about anger, money worries or jealousy, there is something here to ponder, and you will probably also learn how to laugh at yourself and accept yourself because God accepts you. *Grace (Eventually)* is a wonderful book to give to someone with a poor self-image, who would like to believe but is too afraid to trust. As Anne Lamott testifies over and over again, the movement of grace heals and changes us.

In *Grace (Eventually)* Anne demonstrates what she advocates in *Bird by Bird*. This is writing that looks effortless but is crafted with care, as she paints characters for us such as her adopted grandmother Gertrud, includes dialogue that brings the situation to life, focuses on small happenings that are filled with meaning when we pay attention.

It is not accurate to say that she is practising what she preaches because there is nothing preachy about Anne Lamott's writing. It is stories told, insight offered and wisdom shared. There are stories of forgiveness and of the struggle involved to give and receive it. She describes a dog walk on a baking hot day, the rubbish lying around, the people she met and the sudden awareness that there was also beauty present. Suddenly she recognized the truth of Paul's words in his letter to the Romans that where sin abounds grace abounds even more (Romans 5.20). It is almost as though grace is best displayed against the background of sin, and even though it comes in small doses, it transforms everything with insight, hope and faith.

Big issues

Anne is not afraid to tackle big questions such as abortion and assisted dying, remaining honest and personal so that her voice makes its own contribution to a more nuanced debate around these topics. She writes about the difficult relationship she had with her mother, without bitterness or blame and trying to see her point of view. All the same, it was hard for Anne to forgive her, even though she was encouraged to do so by close friends and relatives. She writes, 'I did it my way, slowly, badly, authentically, eventually scattering her ashes, with deep grief, a year and a half after she died.'[6] This is a picture of the 'forgiveness school' that is life in all its untidy, messy and unfinished condition. She points out that 'faith and grace will not look as they do in Bible stories, will not involve angels, flames, or harps'.[7] As well as spiritual WD-40, Anne likens grace to water wings and to ribbons of fresh air in tight scary rooms in one of her other books.[8]

I want dessert

Anne Lamott, like Marilynne Robinson, is fond of the word 'soul' and writes about the human soul in compelling ways. If you are looking for Christian doctrine explained in biblical terminology you will not find it in Anne's writings. What she is doing is telling stories of lives coping with muddle and sometimes mess, and showing how the great Christian themes of hope, love, redemption and mercy actually work in practice.

Traveling Mercies tells in exuberant detail how Anne learned to shine the light of faith on the darkest parts of ordinary life, exposing surprising pockets of meaning and hope, while her most recent book, *Almost Everything: Notes on hope*, tackles the paradox of life head on. There is death and there is life. Love and goodness and the world's humanity are the reasons we have hope, in spite of the other things around us. This can be confusing, but it is a real issue for anyone prepared to reflect on life beyond our own narrow horizon. How can we be happy when children are dying of hunger, for example? As we look around, it does not seem that light is making much progress, despite what we say about God's redeeming love, yet the truth is that we have been redeemed and saved by love. Love is why we have hope.[9]

The book has a powerful chapter on hate and the damage it does to our humanity. Anne is adamant that we must not give in to hate and its destructive power over us. Whether it is hatred of politicians or of close family, the cry is to surrender hate so that it cannot have the last word, for we do not know when life will end. Quoting Wendell Berry, 'Be joyful though you have considered all the facts', she comments, 'I want to have dessert.'[10] She makes this concrete by describing her relationship with an uncle who for years held her at arm's length and for whom she could find no real love. Towards the end, having recounted her struggle to find a way to relate to him, she says, 'All those years I wished he was the sort of uncle I would miss when he died and now he is.'[11]

Writing is hard

I began with *Bird by Bird*, which has become a mirror to the writing process for me as this book has taken shape. The opening lines are arresting:

I grew up around a father and mother who read every chance they got, who took us to the library every Thursday night to load up on books for the coming week. Most nights after dinner my father stretched out on the couch to read, while my mother sat with her book in the easy chair and the three of us kids each retired to our own private reading stations.[12]

Anne's father was a writer, which she found disconcerting as a child: why didn't he put on a tie and go out to work like other fathers? But her father knew that writing gave him the excuse to do things, to go to places and explore. Writing also motivates the writer to look closely at life 'as it lurches by and tramps around'.[13] He taught Anne to write largely by example, demonstrating to her the importance of writing every day and of reading great books, plays and poetry.

Nevertheless, writing is hard. There is nothing for it but to accept that a first draft is bound to be substandard and the only solution is to stay in the chair and keep writing. *Bird by Bird* tells us how Anne started writing and includes the fantasies around writing as well as the reality of it. She has put down what she has learned along the way as a writer, the things she passes on to her students who want to write too.

Good writing is about telling the truth. Writing itself is a little bit like prayer. First you sit down, and try to sit at approximately the same time each day. Her description of trying to get started reminded me of Archbishop Michael Ramsay's response to the question of how long he prayed each day. 'About two minutes,' he said to the shocked interviewer. 'But it takes me twenty-eight to get there,' he added.[14] Anne comments that writing is a matter of persistence and faith and hard work: 'So you might as well just go ahead and get started.'[15]

Finding our voice

Another thing that stops writers from writing is distractions in the head and, just like with prayer, we need to find a way of putting them down so that they cannot interrupt. Perfectionism will certainly ruin efforts to write, and perfectionism in spiritual things lies in setting ourselves up to fail, so we need to learn to see ourselves as God sees us. This will relieve us of any perfectionism and it will also free us to keep going.

Anne writes about plot, character and landscape. Her chapter on the moral point of view uses humour to explain the difference between moralizing and having a moral point of view that is a passionate caring inside. She urges writers to write about the things that are important to them, but to consider carefully whether these things are also important to others. Writing about God means avoiding one-dimensional moralizing.

One of the final chapters is about finding your own voice, and this also reminded me of spirituality. We cannot grow if we are trying to become someone other than ourselves. When her students ask yet again why writing matters, Anne says that it is because of the spirit, because of the heart.

Anne Lamott's thoughts on writing are good companions to set beside Sarah Clarkson's thoughts on reading, for the two are complementary and both have their place as spiritual practices. Writing and reading have always played an important part in Christian identity and expression. They both decrease our sense of isolation. They deepen and widen and expand our sense of life: they feed the soul. Perhaps that is why God the Word led people to write God's words down.

Have you ever prayed a prayer like this:

Hi, God. I'm just a mess. It is all hopeless. What else is new? I would be sick of me, if I were you, but miraculously you are not. I know I have no control over other people's lives, and I hate this. Yet I believe that if I accept this and surrender, you will meet me wherever I am. Wow. Can this be true? If so, how is this afternoon – say two-ish? Thank you in advance for your company and blessings. You have never once let me down. Amen.[16]

Down-to-earth prayer

This is the essence of Anne Lamott's little book on how to pray. *Help, Thanks, Wow* focuses on prayer in a down-to-earth and practical way. She prays a lot – 'many times a day' – and this being a hard planet, it is all she can do.[17] There are a good many things to pray for: health, happiness for her friends and for their children, that the leaders of the world will act for the common good, that aid will quickly reach those who need it, and for her cat, which is dying, to have an easy death.

This opens up a discussion of being 'big in prayer' and expecting God to care for the little things as well as the planet itself. Of prayer she says, 'I want to tell God what to do . . . But it wouldn't work.'[18] This is about praying for God's will to be done and leaving the detail of how up to him. For some people, this is not an adequate approach to prayer, but for others it is where they have landed in walking by faith and not by sight. In *Help, Thanks, Wow*, Anne has some interesting things to say about imagination, a subject that has recurred in the discussions about writing in this book. She writes:

And imagination is from God. It is part of the way we understand the world. I think it's okay to imagine God and grace the best you can. Some of the stuff we imagine engages and connects and calls for the very best in us to come out. Other imaginings disengage us and shut us down. My understanding is that you get to choose which of your thoughts to go with.[19]

Anne's God-box

Praying prayers of help will probably mean being part of the answer. Anne's three great truths that she argues we must own up to if we are going to recognize the presence of God each day in our lives are that we are so ruined, we are so loved and we are in charge of so little.

How may we learn to let go in prayer? Anne offers a simple tool which she calls a God-box. It requires a physical container and in it she places a paper note on which she has written the name of the person she is distressed about. That distress might be longing for healing or release from trouble, or it might be rage against that person or fear around them. It is about letting go, and Anne is confident that the answer will come sooner or later, and when it does it may not be how we'd like things and it will certainly not be about us and our contribution. But it will mean that we have let go and recognized that we cannot fix it. With her characteristic humour she quotes an old riddle: 'What is the difference between you and God? Answer: God never thinks he's you.'[20] We take ourselves off the hook and put God on the hook, where he belongs – a sharp reminder of the literal hook of the crucifixion. And with that, and a reminder to say thank you when the answer comes, the book ends.

Key themes
- God in the midst of life's mess
- Grace
- The authority of experience
- The struggles of writing
- Life's paradoxes
- Humour helps

Questions and action points
- Do you have a favourite metaphor for grace or a story that illustrates it perfectly for you?

- Anne Lamott does not make frequent mention of Jesus in her writing, though the Christian gospel of good news is everywhere acknowledged. Do you find this disconcerting or a helpful way of connecting faith to daily life?
- How important is a sense of humour in communicating essential truths? Does Anne Lamott's funny side draw you in or strike you as flippant and/or distracting?
- Is life a paradox in your experience? Where do you find yourself resisting the complexities and contradictions of daily life and faith?
- Anne is very open about her mental health and character failings. How helpful do you find this approach to writing about faith?
- Anne writes about the things that screw us up: damaged parenting, poverty, abuse, addiction, disease and so on. Some writers would simply name these as the effects of sin in a fallen world. How does Anne Lamott's way of writing open up a conversation with people for whom 'sin' is an alien word?
- What has helped you get through dark times?

Select writings

Almost Everything: Notes on hope (New York: Riverhead Books, 2018).

Bird by Bird: Some instructions on writing and life (New York: Anchor Books, 1995).

Grace (Eventually): Thoughts on faith (New York: Riverhead Books, 2007).

Hallelujah Anyway: Rediscovering mercy (New York: Riverhead Books, 2017).

Hard Laughter (New York: Viking Press, 1980).

Help, Thanks, Wow (London: Hodder and Stoughton, 2013).

Operating Instructions: A journal of my son's first year (New York: Anchor Books, 1993).

Plan B: Further thoughts on faith (New York: Riverhead Books, 2005).

Traveling Mercies: Some thoughts on faith (New York: Riverhead Books, 2000).

'12 truths I have learned from life and writing', TED talk, April 2017, <https://www.ted.com/talks/anne_lamott_12_truths_i_learned _from_life_and_writing?language=en>.

Film

Bird by Bird with Annie: A film portrait of writer Anne Lamott (Freida Lee Mock, 1999).

12

Mary Oliver: listening convivially to the world

'Thank you for reading the poem in your sermon. Can we have more poems please? We like poems.' The person who spoke to me at the end of the morning service went on to say that she had kept the copy of the last poem I had given the congregation in her bedside Bible to read every now and again. It was a poem about prayer.

Poetry and prayer

It has to be admitted, nevertheless, that poetry does not do it for everyone. Poetry is divisive, and for some it will forever remain a closed book. When so much of the Bible is in poetic form, however, it may be worth taking another look for those who shy away from the genre, perhaps imagining that they don't have a poetic line in their being. This may have a lot to do with poetry having been destroyed by inadequate treatment at school, and for some there has never been a recovery from this negative experience. Happily, I was encouraged to write poetry as a child and, in addition, the task of being given poems to learn meant that poetry became something positive and fun. Later on, discovering 'grown-up' poems through people who loved the genre and realizing in one of those penny-dropping moments that the Bible was full of poetry, my love for it was sealed for ever.

There are poets who write explicitly Christian verse and there are poets who write poetry who happen to be Christians. Mary Oliver's poetry cannot be read without hearing whispers of transcendence at every turn, but few of her poems are directly concerned with Christian doctrine or narrative. Prayer appears a good deal, but perhaps not in the form we are used to in church. For anyone who has asked what it means to 'pray without ceasing' (1 Thessalonians 5.17), Mary Oliver's poetry offers a rich store of material for meditation.

Little allelujahs

Mary Oliver died early in 2019, aged 83, as I was writing this book. She was one of America's best and most loved poets and the recipient of multiple awards, including the Pulitzer Prize. Her first book of poems was published in 1963 when she was 28: *No Voyage, and Other Poems.*

Mary Oliver published a great deal more in the years that followed, both poetry and prose, and she also taught many students about the craft of writing. Her prose often describes and analyses the writing process and includes observations about the world. She was a private person and did not give many interviews, nor did she disclose in her work great details about herself, compared to other writers represented here such as Kathleen Norris. There are numerous articles about her and her poems are quoted often. The former Vice-President of the USA, Joe Biden, read her poem 'Wild geese', for example, at the 9/11 memorial in New York. In addition, she often did readings herself, and examples of her reading her own poems may be found online.

Mary Oliver's poetry and approach to writing poetry invite further reflection on the relationship between poetry and prayer and, in addition, what poetry can do for us in terms of being alive to the world. Mary Oliver was certainly someone who was fully alive. She noted that a mind that is lively and inquiring, compassionate, curious, angry, full of music and full of feeling is a mind full of possible poetry. Poetry, she added, is a life-cherishing force. And it requires vision – a faith.[1]

What is it about her poetry that has such a wide appeal? Mary speaks of poetry as a communal ritual – that is, poetry is written for anybody and everybody. Some of us write poetry and keep it hidden from the world, so perhaps this points to another similarity with prayer. Some prayers are intensely private, but there is a corpus of prayer, some of it very ancient, that is available for anyone and everyone to borrow and make their own. Mark Oakley comments that Mary's poems are both intimately moving and publicly poised.[2]

Mary Oliver said that she wanted the 'I' in her poems to be the reader, and I believe she achieves that over and over again; this is what strikes those who read her. We are invited to become the subject, seeing, feeling and responding. When I first heard her read 'The first time Percy came back' online, I found myself weeping. The poem touched a loss and a yearning for my own long-deceased dog Noah. It was dreamlike, vivid, real – as she says of Percy's appearing in the poem – but it had become my experience as well as hers. All good poetry does this in the same way that Scripture addresses us, and we find ourselves and our story within the big story that it narrates.

Waking up to life

Born in 1935, Mary Oliver had what she called 'an insufficient childhood'. She used to walk around the woods of Ohio and this practice was her salvation. She felt she was saved by poetry and the beauty of the world. She never set out without a pen and a notebook, and as she walked she wrote.

Some of her poems urge us to wake up to the one life we have been given and to live it wholeheartedly. For her, poetry helped her to do this well. It is not as though poetry is an easy life to choose, all the same. In *A Poetry Handbook: A prose guide to understanding and writing poetry*, published in 1994, she acknowledges the hard graft that goes into writing, especially revising a poem. *A Poetry Handbook* shows how competently Mary Oliver inhabits her craft and how deftly she communicates it. It represents the summary of what she taught her students on her poetry-writing courses.

Even for the non-poet, there is much to ponder about writing and the spiritual life here. For example, rarely does Mary Oliver produce a complete poem in one go but has to revise repeatedly. Rewriting is hard work, hard work, hard work, she confesses.[3] How might this relate to the spiritual life, I wonder? The New Testament talks about being refined like gold and is clear that we do not change overnight into the finished product as complete human beings. Salvation is both now and not yet.

Poetry and prayer

In the same volume, Mary Oliver argues that poetry can connect the conscious mind with the heart. All the great teachers on prayer insist that prayer needs to get us out of our heads and down into our hearts in order that God can do God's work in us. Similarly, teachers on prayer discuss whether prayer can really be taught, and Mary says of poetry that while it cannot all be taught, there is a great deal that can and must be learned.[4] She goes on to say that poets are born, but that is not to say that there is nothing to learn.

Can the same be said of prayer? If it is true that we are all born able to cry out to God in prayer, then prayer may be said to be innate and not learned. Anyone can pray. As with poetry, however, there is always more to learn about prayer, and the key to both is practice. Those who teach the writing of poetry advise would-be poets to read other poets as much as possible. While we may be lured into read-ing too many books about prayer instead of praying ourselves, there is great gain in absorbing the wisdom of teachers of prayer, both past and present.

Rules for writing poetry

In the chapter titled 'Free verse', Mary Oliver remarks that free verse is, of course, not 'free', but there are hidden rules, even if they are being broken at every point. A poem may be free from metrical design, for instance, but it still has some kind of design. In prayer, there are no rules about right and wrong ways to pray, but there are some givens, such as when we pray we enter into a dialogue with someone who is bigger than we are. We may call him *Abba*, Father, or we may stick to 'Higher Power', but there is an otherness about God that includes being greater than we are in every way.

Poetry is language that is 'spontaneous and impulsive, but it is also composed, considered, appropriate and effective even after reading a hundred times'.[5] In the way Mary Oliver describes poetic language here, there seems to be an echo of liturgical prayer, for example from the *Book of Common Prayer* or many of the psalms. She has said that her poems grew shorter as she went along. There was a paring back, which led to what one critic called her 'lean lines'. This represents the hard work and the need for courage in getting rid of words that do not work. This, too, reminds me of the need to let go of excess baggage as we grow older and of the experience of saying less in prayer that many own may be part of that. It is as if there is no need to run on and on in prayer, for the objective has become one of abiding in God's pres-ence. Words can sometimes get in the way, and we need fewer of them to communicate with God.

For someone who is acclaimed as teaching us how to live, it is noteworthy that Mary Oliver's poems are far more likely to be about a snake, a dog or a heron than a human being. There are few people in her poems, especially the early ones. Later she is more reflective about her own experiences, but always in relation to the natural world. A whole book *Dog Songs*, for example, is about the dogs who shared her life over the years.[6] Deceptively simple, her observations about her dogs' behaviour and their relationships with her invite us to live with more gratitude, generosity and freedom.

She does not only choose beautiful creatures to extol in poetry. Along with snakes, already mentioned, there are box turtles, hermit crabs and moths. In one poem she says it doesn't have to be the blue iris that leads us into prayer; it might just as well be 'weeds in a vacant lot'.[7]

Place and poetry

Place was very important to Mary Oliver and pervades her poetry. From the Ohio woods of her childhood to her long stay as an adult in and around Provincetown at the far tip of Cape Cod, Massachusetts, geography and the natural world formed the focus of her attention and provided the material for her writing. Her awareness of the world around shaped her as a person and in turn infused her writing. She lived in Provincetown for 50 years and loved it deeply. Once again, references to Thoreau have been found by those who have analysed her work and have also found points of comparison with other influential literary figures.

Naturally her environment changed a great deal over that time, and Mary Oliver explores the challenges and opportunities we all face in the midst of a changing and uncertain world. She is not bitter about the challenge change presents, however, painful though it clearly must have been, and it is gratitude that dominates her attitude to the world. Nevertheless, she finds the damage to the natural world disturbing and bad for human beings. One of the longest titles of a poem by her runs 'What was once the largest shopping center [sic] in Northern Ohio was built where there had been a pond I used to visit every summer afternoon'. Do we really need all this stuff? the poem asks.

Like Kathleen Norris, Annie Dillard and others, the natural world shaped Mary Oliver's vision. Like them, she had the gift of paying attention, which, she said, is the beginning of devotion. In an interview with Krista Tippett for 'On being', she spoke about 'listening convivially to the world'.[8] In *A Poetry Handbook* she insisted that the poet must not only write the poem, but must also 'scrutinise' the world intensely. Failure to do so will result in a 'thin poem'.[9] Perhaps it is also true that failure to live life deeply and reflectively will result in a 'thin' life – that is, a life lived on the surface, constantly missing the point. Although this kind of patient looking may be a gift of personality, all the writers represented here suggest that it is also a skill that may be honed with frequent practice.

A vocation to love the world

These twin themes of rejoicing in the life we have been given and paying attention to what is all around us appear over and over again in Mary Oliver's poetry and supply both its pervasive sense of gratitude and its urgency to live every day fully. In the opening poem of her collection *Thirst*, she explains that her whole work is to love the world.[10] In a poem called 'The sweetness of dogs', she watches the moon outside with her dog Percy. She sits there in happy companionship with him and thinks how grateful she is for the moon's perfect beauty and the richness of loving the world. Then as if to reinforce the moment, Percy leans in and she too feels loved.[11]

Her collection entitled *Why I Wake Early* has a quotation from George Herbert at the beginning: 'Lord! Who hath praise enough?' She is constantly exclaiming at the wonder and extra-ordinary beauty of seemingly ordinary things, urging us to wake up and see for ourselves. She tells how she wanted to write a poem about the world that had nothing 'fancy' in it, but found it impossible.[12]

The world throws its question to us each new day: 'Here you are, alive. What is your response to that?' The Jewish proverb 'Did you enjoy my world?', mentioned in connection with Sarah Clarkson in Chapter 4, would elicit a resounding 'Yes!' from Mary Oliver. After all, she wants us to think of her poems as 'lit-tle allelujahs'.[13] 'What does it mean that the earth is so beautiful? And what shall I do about it? What is the gift that I should bring to the world? What is the life that I should live?'[14] Such questions challenge us to live each day as if it were the only one gifted to us.

Describing her early morning routine, Mary Oliver tells how, hav-ing made her coffee, she goes from window to window lifting the sash. I do this too, but how often do I look out and take in what is there? Do I pause, like the poet, to watch the way the light changes in all its subtlety and notice that it is not simply a pink sky but also contains tangerine, apricot and lavender?[15] I fear I may be unseeing, my mind already on the next thing I have to do even as the curtains are moving back.

Thirsting for God

Mary Oliver's final collection of poems, *Thirst*, addresses many Chris-tian themes. She exemplifies the quotation from Marilynne Robin-son's *Gilead*, that 'nothing true can be said about God from a posture of defence',[16] and her questioning approach to life is full of resonance with Christian faith without being dogmatic. Her openness to the way the world addresses our inner life allows for an exploration of the way poetry affects people in general, as well as how her poems strike particular chords.

Now that she has died, there is a special poignancy in reading her poem about her own death. She does not lament that life will be over or express regrets that there are certain things she will not now be able to do. Instead she plays with the metaphor of marriage, first imagining herself as the bride who was 'married to amazement' and then putting herself in the place of the groom who takes his bride – now the world, into his arms.[17]

She has helped me to reimagine a new dimension of holiness. This earth is God's arena and we stand on holy ground. Seeing the world through God's eyes has been a recurring theme among these writers, who have used their gifts with words to express wonder, love and praise. It is part of our calling as human beings to worship the Creator through the created world in which we have been placed and into which the Word took flesh and dwelt among us. Mary Oliver's words carry an Advent-like message to pay attention to the world, to stay awake and alive to what it conveys.

Key themes

- Gratitude
- Paying attention
- The wonder of the world
- The amazing fact of each new day
- Our relationship with animals

Questions and action points

- Mary Oliver insists we cannot separate the world's appearance and actions from morality and valour. Thus the butterfly gives us the idea of transcendence, the forest shows us not the inert but the aspiring, and in water that departs forever and forever returns we experience eternity.[18] Are there features of the natural world that lead you to similar allusions? What are they and of what do they remind you?

- Where do you go to listen 'convivially' to the world? If this is a new thought, try to notice your surroundings and allow enough time to take in the details of a cloud, a tree or an insect.
- What aspects of poetry that are compared with prayer in this chapter resonate with you the most?
- How would you answer God's question, 'Did you enjoy my world?' in the Jewish story?
- Does publishing a book of poems solely about one's pet dogs seem appropriate to you? If you are a dog lover or owner, try writing a poem about a dog you have known. If you are not, choose something that gives you joy and write a poem about it.
- Unlike Ann Lewin's prayer poems, which often refer directly to the Christian story, Mary Oliver tends towards language that evokes the spiritual without necessarily including religious content. Does this matter to you? Do you know of anyone for whom this approach might be a bridge to the spiritual life?
- The critic Stanley Kunitz commented that Mary Oliver's poems read like 'a blessing'.[19] Can you recall a poem that has blessed you? A psalm or a song from Scripture? How could you cultivate a deeper sense of gratitude for your life today?

Select writings

Devotions: The selected poems of Mary Oliver (East Rutherford: Penguin, 2017).

Dog Songs (East Rutherford: Penguin, 2013).

Long Life: Essays and other writings (Boston: Da Capo Press, 2004).

New and Selected Poems (Boston: Beacon Press, 1992).

No Voyage, and Other Poems (Boston: Houghton Mifflin, 1965).

A Poetry Handbook: A prose guide to understanding and writing poetry (New York: Harcourt, Inc, 1994).

Thirst (Northumberland: Bloodaxe, 2007).

A Thousand Mornings (London: Corsair, 2012).
Upstream: Selected essays (East Rutherford: Penguin, 2016).
Why I Wake Early (Boston: Beacon Press, 2004).
Wild Geese (Northumberland: Bloodaxe, 2004).

Websites

<www.maryoliver.beacon.org>
<www.poetryfoundation.org/poets/mary-oliver>

Notes

Introduction

1 Madeleine L'Engle, 'The Expanding Universe', Newbery Award Acceptance Speech, August 1963.

2 G. K. Chesterton, *The Autobiography of G. K. Chesterton* (San Francisco: Ignatius Press, 2006), p. 99.

3 Mary Oliver, *Upstream: Selected essays* (London: Penguin, 2016), p. 9.

4 Dallas Willard, *The Spirit of the Disciplines* (London: Hodder and Stoughton, 1988), p. 31.

5 Marilynne Robinson, *Gilead* (London: Picador, 2006), p. 177.

6 Malcolm Guite, *The Word in the Wilderness* (Norwich: Canterbury Press, 2014), p. 83.

7 See Richard Harries, *Haunted by Christ: Modern writers and the struggle for faith* (London: SPCK, 2018).

8 Stefan Bollmann, *Women Who Write Are Dangerous* (revised edition) (New York: Abbeville Press, 2018).

9 W. H. Auden, cited in Humphrey Carpenter, *W. H. Auden: A biography* (London: Faber and Faber, 2011), p. xiii.

1 Kathleen Norris: everyday mysteries

1 Kathleen Norris, *The Quotidian Mysteries: Laundry, liturgy and 'women's work'* (New Jersey: Paulist Press, 1998), p. 22.

2 Kathleen Norris, *Amazing Grace: A vocabulary of faith* (Oxford: Lion, 1998), p. 19.

3 Norris, *Amazing Grace*, p. 218.

4 Norris, *Amazing Grace*, p. 219.

5 Norris, *Amazing Grace*, p. 14.

6 Kathleen Norris, *Dakota: A spiritual geography* (New York: Ticknor and Fields, 1993), p. 2.

7 Norris, *Dakota*, p. 2.

8 Norris, *Amazing Grace*, p. 226.

9 Norris, *Amazing Grace*, pp. 73ff.

10 Angela Tilby, *The Seven Deadly Sins: Their origin in the spiritual teaching of Evagrius the Hermit* (London: SPCK, 2009).

11 'Flowers in the Desert. Homiletics Interview: Kathleen Norris', 'Homiletics Online', 2011, <https://www.homileticsonline.com/subscriber/interviews/norris.asp>.

12 Norris, *The Noonday Demon: A modern woman's struggle with soul-weariness* (Oxford: Lion Hudson, 2008, 2009), p. 208.

2 Alison Morgan: following Jesus

1 Alison Morgan, *Dante and the Medieval Other World* (Cambridge: Cambridge University Press, 2007, first published 1990).

2 Alison Morgan, *The Wild Gospel: Bringing truth to life* (Oxford: Monarch, 2004), p. 4.

3 Morgan, *The Wild Gospel*, p. 5.

4 'Flowers in the Desert. Homiletics Interview: Kathleen Norris', 'Homiletics Online', 2011, <https://www.homileticsonline.com/subscriber/interviews/norris.asp>.

5 Morgan, *The Wild Gospel*, p. 7.

6 Morgan, *The Wild Gospel*, pp. 72ff.

7 Morgan, *The Wild Gospel*, p. 83.

8 Alison Morgan, *The Word on the Wind: Renewing confidence in the gospel* (Oxford: Monarch, 2011).

9 Morgan, *The Word on the Wind*, p. 1.

10 Alison Morgan, *Following Jesus: The plural of disciple is Church* (Searcy: ReSource, 2015), p. 48.

11 Morgan, *The Wild Gospel*, p. 122.

12 Morgan, *The Word on the Wind*, p. 231.

13 Alison Morgan, 'A Bird's Eye View', *ReSource*, March 2014, <https://www.alisonmorgan.co.uk/Articles/Birds&theSpiritualLifeAJM.pdf>.

14 Morgan, 'A Bird's Eye View'.

15 Alison Morgan, *The Word of God: What does it mean?* (Searcy: ReSource, 2008), p. 10. See Chapter 5 for Annie Dillard.

16 Alison Morgan, 'Summaries of useful books', <https://www.alisonmorgan.co.uk/Books.htm>.

17 Morgan, *The Wild Gospel*, p. 7.

3 Ann Lewin: watching for the kingfisher

1 Ann Lewin, 'Disclosure', *Watching for the Kingfisher* (new and enlarged edition) (Norwich: Canterbury Press, 2009), p. 31.

2 Mark Oakley, *The Splash of Words: Believing in poetry* (Norwich: Canterbury Press, 2016), p. xxix.

3 Ann Lewin, in conversation with Liz Hoare, September 2018.

4 Lewin, 'Uphill journey', *Watching for the Kingfisher*, p. 58.

5 For example, Robert Llewellyn (ed.), *Julian: Woman of our day* (London: Darton, Longman and Todd, 1985).

6 Julian of Norwich, *Revelations of Divine Love* (Victoria, Australia: Penguin, 1966), ch. 39.

7 Julian of Norwich, *Revelations of Divine Love*, ch. 59.

8 Julian of Norwich, *Revelations of Divine Love*, ch. 29.

9 Lewin, 'For my salvation', *Watching for the Kingfisher*, p. 56.

10 Ann Lewin, *Seasons of Grace: Inspirational resources for the Christian year* (Norwich: Canterbury Press, 2011), p. 223.

11 Lewin, *Seasons of Grace*, pp. 36–8.

12 Lewin, *Seasons of Grace*, p. 38.

13 Lewin, *Seasons of Grace*, p. 38.

14 Ann Lewin, *Love Is the Meaning: Growing in faith with Julian of Norwich* (Norwich: Canterbury Press, 2006), p. 25.

4 Sarah Clarkson: for the love of books

1 C. S. Lewis, *The Four Loves* (Glasgow: Fount, 1980), p. 62.

2 Sarah Clarkson, *Book Girl* (Illinois: Tyndale Momentum, 2018), p. 108.

3 Clarkson, *Book Girl*, p. 37.

4 Clarkson, *Book Girl*, pp. 42–3.

5 Clarkson, *Book Girl*, pp. 93–4.

6 Clarkson, *Book Girl*, p. 96.

5 Annie Dillard: the world is charged with the grandeur of God

1 Annie Dillard, *Pilgrim at Tinker Creek* (New York: Bantam Doubleday Dell, 1974).

2 Annie Dillard, *The Writing Life* (New York: HarperCollins, 1989), p. 4.

3 Dillard, *The Writing Life*, pp. 58–9.

4 Marilynne Robinson, 'The Nature of Love', *The Washington Post*, 24 June 2007, <http://www.washingtonpost.com/wp-dyn/content/article/2007/06/21/AR2007062102058.html>.

5 Dillard, *Pilgrim at Tinker Creek*, p. 8.

6 Annie Dillard, *Mornings Like This* (New York: HarperCollins, 1995), p. ix, author's note.

7 Dillard, *Mornings Like This*, p. 59.

8 Dillard, *Pilgrim at Tinker Creek*, p. 6.

9 Dillard, *Pilgrim at Tinker Creek*, p. 6.

10 Annie Dillard, <www.anniedillard.com/>.

11 Annie Dillard Official Website, Curriculum Vitae, <http://www.anniedillard.com/curriculum-vitae.html>.

12 Quoted in Eugene Peterson, *The Contemplative Pastor: Returning to the art of spiritual direction* (Grand Rapids: Eerdmans, 1989), p. 80.

13 Peterson, *The Contemplative Pastor*, p. 70.

14 Annie Dillard, *Holy the Firm* (New York: Harper and Row, 1977), p. 1.

15 Dillard, *Holy the Firm*, p. 49.

16 Dillard, *Holy the Firm*, p. 71.

17 Prayer by Catherine of Genoa. Source unknown.

18 Peterson, *The Contemplative Pastor*, p. 68.

19 Peterson, *The Contemplative Pastor*, p. 68.

20 Dillard, *Holy the Firm*, p. 22.

21 Peterson, *The Contemplative Pastor*, p. 77.

22 Annie Dillard, *Teaching a Stone to Talk*, quoted in Peterson, *The Contemplative Pastor*, p. 79.

23 Peterson, *The Contemplative Pastor*, p. 80.

24 Annie Dillard, *An American Childhood* (New York: Harper and Row, 1987), p. 63.

25 Dillard, *An American Childhood*, p. 66.

26 Dillard, *The Writing Life*, p. 78.

27 Dillard, *The Writing Life*, p. 73.

28 Dillard, *Pilgrim at Tinker Creek*, p. 79.

29 Dillard, *Pilgrim at Tinker Creek*, p. 81.

30 Dillard, *Pilgrim at Tinker Creek*, p. 8.

31 Peterson, *The Contemplative Pastor*, p. 85.

6 Margaret Guenther: spiritual midwifery

1 Margaret Guenther, *Holy Listening* (London: Darton, Longman and Todd, 1992), p. 1.

2 Guenther, *Holy Listening*, p. 7.

3 Guenther, *Holy Listening*, ch. 2.

4 Barbara Brennan and Joan Rattner Heilman (eds), *The Complete Book of Midwifery* (Boston: E. P. Dutton and Co., 1977).

5 See also <www.spiritualityandpractice.com>.

6 Margaret Guenther, *Toward Holy Ground: Spiritual direction for the second half of life* (Cambridge: Cowley Publications, 1995), p. 131.

7 Guenther, *Toward Holy Ground*, p. 135.

8 Margaret Guenther, *Walking Home: From Eden to Emmaus* (Harrisburg: Morehouse Publishing, 2011), p. 56.

9 Guenther, *Walking Home*, p. 130.

7 Sister Margaret Magdalen: avoiding mediocrity

1 Margaret Magdalen, *Jesus, Man of Prayer* (London: Hodder and Stoughton, 1987), preface.

2 W. E. Sangster, *A Spiritual Check-up* (London: Epworth Press, 1952).

3 Margaret Magdalen, *A Spiritual Check-up: Avoiding mediocrity in the Christian life* (Godalming: Highland, 1990), p. 15.

4 Magdalen, *A Spiritual Check-up*, ch. 3, pp. 18ff.

5 Magdalen, *A Spiritual Check-up*, p. 22.

6 Magdalen, *A Spiritual Check-up*, p. 69.

7 Magdalen, *A Spiritual Check-up*, p. 70.

8 Magdalen, *A Spiritual Check-up*, p. 186.

9 Magdalen, *Jesus, Man of Prayer*, pp. 15–16.

10 Magdalen, *Jesus, Man of Prayer*, p. 27.

11 Teilhard de Chardin, quoted in Magdalen, *Jesus, Man of Prayer*, p. 34.

12 Magdalen, *Jesus, Man of Prayer*, p. 34.

13 Magdalen, *Jesus, Man of Prayer*, p. 85.

14 Magdalen, *Jesus, Man of Prayer*, p. 99.

15 Magdalen, *Jesus, Man of Prayer*, pp. 204–7.

16 Margaret Magdalen, *The Hidden Face of Jesus: Reflections on the emotional life of Christ* (London: Darton, Longman and Todd, 1994), pp. 31–2.

17 Magdalen, *The Hidden Face of Jesus*, p. 32.

18 Gerard Hughes, *God of Surprises* (London: Darton, Longman and Todd, 1987).

19 James Martin, *The Jesuit Guide to (Almost) Everything* (New York: HarperCollins, 2010).

8 Sister Benedicta Ward: with all the saints

1 Attributed to St Augustine of Hippo.

2 Benedicta Ward, *High King of Heaven: Aspects of early English spirituality* (London: Mowbray, 1999), p. xi.

3 Benedicta Ward, *Give Love and Receive the Kingdom* (Brewster: Paraclete Press, 2018).

4 Ward, *Give Love and Receive the Kingdom*, p. v.

5 Benedicta Ward (trans.), 'Moses', *The Sayings of the Desert Fathers: The Alphabet Collection* (London: Mowbray, 1975, 1981), p. 2.

6 Ward, 'Anthony the Great', *The Sayings of the Desert Fathers*, p. 6.

7 Norman Russell (trans.), with introduction by Benedicta Ward, *The Lives of the Desert Fathers* (London: Mowbray, 1980), p. 45.

8 Benedicta Ward (trans.), *The Wisdom of the Desert Fathers* (Oxford: Fairacres Publications, 1975, 1981), p. 178.

9 Ward, 'Joseph of Panephysis', *The Sayings of the Desert Fathers*, p. 7.

10 The Community of St Anselm, <https://www.stanselm.org.uk/>.

11 Anselm, quoted in Ward, *Give Love and Receive the Kingdom*, p. 111.

12 Ward, *Give Love and Receive the Kingdom*, introduction, p. v.

13 Ward, *High King of Heaven*, p. 51.

14 Ward, *High King of Heaven*, p. 96.

15 Ward, *High King of Heaven*, p. 102.

16 Jane Chance (ed.), *Women Medievalists and the Academy* (Madison: University of Wisconsin Press, 2005).

9 Marilynne Robinson: the givenness of things

1 Marilynne Robinson, *When I Was a Child I Read Books* (London: Virago, 2012), p. 85.

2 C. S. Lewis, *An Experiment in Criticism* (Cambridge: Cambridge University Press, 1961), p. 141.

3 Marilynne Robinson, quoted in Lucy Scholes, 'The Givenness of Things Review – Marilynne Robinson's passionate defence of Christianity', *The Guardian*, 16 October 2016, <https://www.theguardian.com/books/2016/oct/16/givenness-of-things-marylinne-robinson-review>.

4 Marilynne Robinson, *Gilead* (London: Virago, 2005), p. 281.

5 Robinson, *Gilead*, p. 96.

6 Marilynne Robinson, *Home* (London: Virago, 2008), p. 176.

7 Marilynne Robinson, *Lila* (London: Virago, 2014), p. 48.

8 Robinson, *Lila*, p. 29.

9 Robinson, *Lila*, p. 131.

10 Robinson, *When I Was a Child I Read Books*, p. 86.

11 Robinson, *When I Was a Child I Read Books*, p. 20.

12 Robinson, *Gilead*, pp. 146ff.

13 Robinson, *Gilead*, p. 147.

14 Robinson, *Gilead*, p. 141.

15 Robinson, *Gilead*, p. 151.

16 Rowan Williams, 'A compelling story of transforming grace', *Church Times*, 1 April 2016, <https://www.churchtimes.co.uk/articles/2016/1-april/books-arts/reading-groups/a-compelling-story-of-transforming-grace>.

17 See Robinson, *When I Was a Child I Read Books*, p. xiv.

18 Krista Tippett, 'The mystery we are', interview with Marilynne Robinson and Marcelo Gleiser, On Being, 8 January 2012, <https://onbeing.org/programs/marilynne-robinson-marcelo-gleiser-the-mystery-we-are/>.

19 Jonathan Edwards, cited at <https://quotefancy.com/quote/1173840/Jonathan-Edwards-Nature-is-God-s-greatest-evangelist>.

10 Barbara Brown Taylor: struggles with the Church

1 Barbara Brown Taylor, *The Gate of Heaven: Preaching the Gospel of Matthew* (Norwich: Canterbury Press, 2016), p. viii.

2 Barbara Brown Taylor, *An Altar in the World: Finding the sacred beneath our feet* (Norwich: Canterbury Press, 2009), p. 31.

3 Brown Taylor, *An Altar in the World*, p. 15.

4 Barbara Brown Taylor, *The Preaching Life: Living out your vocation* (Cambridge, MA: Cowley Publications, 1993), p. 8.

5 Brown Taylor, *The Preaching Life*, p. 8.

6 Brown Taylor, *The Preaching Life*, p. 10.

7 Brown Taylor, *The Preaching Life*, p. 21.

8 Barbara Brown Taylor, *Leaving Church: A memoir of faith* (Norwich: Canterbury Press, 2009), p. 195.

9 Brown Taylor, *Leaving Church*, p. 168.

10 Brown Taylor, *Leaving Church*, p. 111.

11 Brown Taylor, *The Gate of Heaven*, pp. 55–60.

12 Brown Taylor, *The Preaching Life*, p. 56.

13 Brown Taylor, *The Preaching Life*, p. 58.

14 Barbara Brown Taylor, *When God Is Silent: Divine language beyond words* (Norwich: Canterbury Press, 1996), p. 35.

15 Brown Taylor, *The Preaching Life*, p. 92.

16 Brown Taylor, *An Altar in the World*, p. 150.

17 Barbara Brown Taylor, *Learning to Walk in the Dark* (Norwich: Canterbury Press, 2015), p. 15.

11 Anne Lamott: life in forgiveness school

1 Agnieszka Tennant, '"Jesusy" Anne Lamott', *Christianity Today*, 1 January 2003, <https://www.christianitytoday.com/ct/2003/january/8.56.html>.

2 Anne Lamott, *Traveling Mercies: Some thoughts on faith* (New York: Riverhead Books, 2000), p. 3.

3 Anne Lamott, *Grace (Eventually): Thoughts on faith* (New York: Riverhead Books, 2007), p. 2.

4 Lamott, *Grace (Eventually)*, pp. 1ff.

5 Lamott, *Grace (Eventually)*, p. 51.

6 Lamott, *Grace (Eventually)*, p. 229.

7 Lamott, *Grace (Eventually)*, p. 246.

8 Anne Lamott, *Help, Thanks, Wow* (London: Hodder and Stoughton, 2013), p. 5.

9 Anne Lamott, *Almost Everything: Notes on hope* (New York: Riverhead Books, 20), pp. 2–3.

10 Lamott, *Almost Everything*, p. 84.

11 Lamott, *Almost Everything*, p. 182.

12 Anne Lamott, *Bird by Bird: Some instructions on writing and life* (New York: Anchor Books, 1995), p. xi.

13 Lamott, *Bird by Bird*, p. xii.

14 Attributed to Michael Ramsay. Source unknown.

15 Lamott, *Bird by Bird*, p. 7.

16 Lamott, *Help, Thanks, Wow*, p. 34.

17 Lamott, *Help, Thanks, Wow*, p. 1.

18 Lamott, *Help, Thanks, Wow*, p. 16.

19 Lamott, *Help, Thanks, Wow*, p. 21.

20 Lamott, *Help, Thanks, Wow*, pp. 35–6.

12 Mary Oliver: listening convivially to the world

1 See Mary Oliver, *A Poetry Handbook: A prose guide to understanding and writing poetry* (New York: Harcourt, Inc, 1994).

2 Mark Oakley, *The Splash of Words: Believing in poetry* (Norwich: Canterbury Press, 2016), p. 90.

3 Oliver, *A Poetry Handbook*, p. 111.

4 Oliver, *A Poetry Handbook*, p. 1.

5 Oliver, *A Poetry Handbook*, p. 67.

6 Mary Oliver, *Dog Songs* (East Rutherford: Penguin, 2013).

7 Mary Oliver, 'Praying', *Thirst* (Northumberland: Bloodaxe, 2007), p. 37.

8 Krista Tippett, 'Mary Oliver: Listening to the world', On Being, 5 February 2015, <https://onbeing.org/programs/mary -oliver-listening-to-the-world-jan2019/>.

9 Oliver, *A Poetry Handbook*, p. 99.

10 Oliver, *Thirst*, p. 1.

11 Oliver, 'The sweetness of dogs', *Dog Songs*, p. 61.

12 Oliver, 'This world', *Why I Wake Early*, p. 27.

13 Mary Oliver, *Long Life: Essays and other writings* (Boston: Da Capo Press, 2004), p. xiv.

14 Oliver, *Long Life*, p. 9.

15 Oliver, *Long Life*, p. 79.

16 Marilynne Robinson, *Gilead* (London: Virago, 2005), p. 177.
17 Mary Oliver, 'When death comes', *New and Selected Poems* (Boston: Beacon Press,1992).
18 Oliver, *Long Life*, p. 25.
19 Citation, Marquette University Honorary Degree conferred on Mary Oliver, 12 November 2012.